There are no born entrepreneurs.
They are born of life's experiences.
—David H. Gilmour

"START UP" IS DEDICATED TO THE ONE
WHO MAKES IT ALL WORTHWHILE,
MY WIFE, JILL.

*The farther backward you can look,
the farther forward you can see.*

—Sir Winston Churchill

First Printing, 2012
Second Printing, 2016
10 9 8 7 6 5 4 3 2

START UP

Don't Predict the Products of the Future,
Create Them!

David H. Gilmour

☥

START UP

Table of Contents

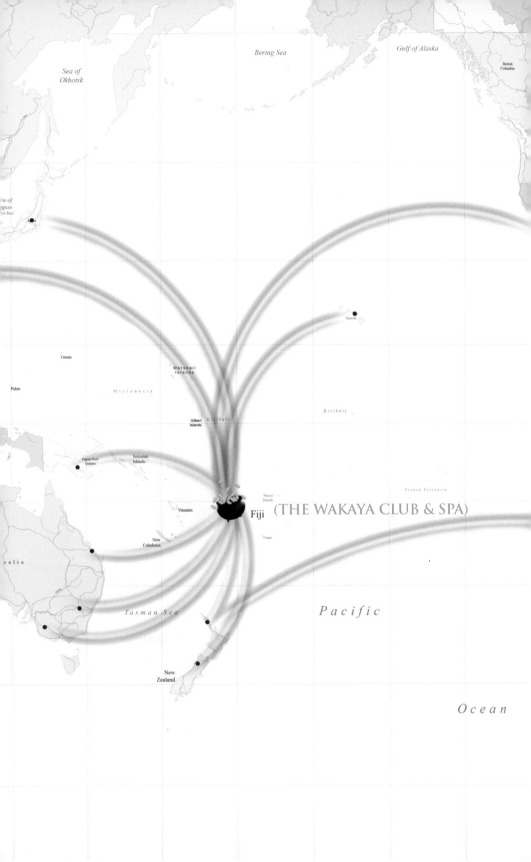

PREFACE

One of my most prized possessions is a portrait by Frank O. Salisbury. "Blood, Sweat, and Tears" hangs in a place of honour in my study.

This is the second home this painting has had since it was commissioned by the Commonwealth Club in 1942 and completed by the artist the following year.

Its first was Number 10 Downing Street.

For as long as I can remember, Winston Churchill has been a hero of mine. I grew up with the stories of my grandfather meeting him in Natal during the Boer War. I also have vivid memories of my father, sitting in the family home in Toronto, listening to the famous radio broadcasts during the Second World War. Later, as a businessman, I came to realize that Churchill embodied qualities in the political realm that I believe to be essential to entrepreneurial success. Politicians seldom provide useful models for anyone embarking on a business career—quite the opposite, usually—but Sir Winston is the exception. His innate ability to command attention, his talent for engaging people's interest, his skill at convincing people that his cause was their cause, his capacity for clearly articulating his thoughts and objectives, his forward thinking, and his decisiveness are aspects of character that would have made him a formidable business leader—had he not been otherwise engaged.

He was courageous, and courage is something upon which, to varying degrees, all entrepreneurs need to draw at one time or another. Churchill's stakes were a good deal higher than most of us are ever called upon to play. But there are times—in the darkest hour of a company as in a country—when conviction is all there is to go on. Whether he was in power or in the political wilderness, Churchill believed: in himself and in his cause. Conviction on its own is never enough, but the other elements that lead to success, in business as in politics, can never work without it.

I was fortunate enough to become a friend of Sir Winston's grandson. The Winston I knew was a chip off the old block: a writer, an adventurer, a politician. Although I am now of an age at which such news cannot be a surprise, Winston's death in 2010 was a blow.

The ancient Egyptian symbol of the ankh, as seen above and

as used throughout this book, represents to me the inter-connectedness of things. I have always had the strong sense that even my earliest memories are linked directly to who I am now—that the story of my life cannot be separated from the story of my entrepreneurial ventures. "Will it be about business or will it be a memoir?" friends have asked when I told them of my plans to write a book. "Both," I reply. In my case, one can't exist without the other.

Good or bad, dark or bright, my experiences have always felt to me as if they have been leading me somewhere. I haven't always been sure where the path is going, but the lifelong habit of trying to learn from the past while trying to peer into the future has made me who I am.

When I was a young man, my father thought that I should take a job in an office—at a brokerage, or an investment firm, or a bank. I was deeply respectful of my father. Much of the advice Dad gave me has shaped my life. But in this instance, even though I couldn't quite see the path I needed to take, I knew instinctively that it lay in another direction.

Similarly, the time I spent as a co-founder of Southern Pacific Hotel Corporation, of Barrick Gold Corporation (the most profitable gold-mining firm in the world), and of Horsham Corporation (which became TrizecHahn Corporation, one of the largest publicly traded REIT companies in North America) was challenging and rewarding. I was, I believe, a valuable partner. But the truth is I was never as consumed by acquisition and management as I am by helping to start things up.

What my experiences have added up to, and what they have helped me create, are the subjects of this book. And while it may be unusual to preface a book with disappointment, there is always some element of sadness that comes with looking back. I am sorry that my old friend, Winston, shall not be ringing me up to let me know what he thinks of what I have written—particularly since, as these pages reveal, his grandfather's life has been such a touchstone for mine.

Were the achievements of Sir Winston Churchill's life to be divided up among the biographies of three men, they would each still seem remarkable. His political life alone is a multi-volume saga. His writing would be prolific for anyone who thought of himself as a writer exclusively. But Sir Winston was not only a politician, and not only a writer. He was also a soldier, a journalist, a military tactician, a wartime leader, a painter, a bricklayer, an historian, and a husband.

All my life I have admired his keen observations. I have often jotted down his famous quotations—sometimes because they are so witty, sometimes because they are so wise, usually because they are both. I'm sure that many business people have encountered the kind of thinking that Churchill summed up so beautifully with his pointed comment: "However beautiful the strategy, you should occasionally look at the results." What sales department would not do well to take as a motto, "Difficulties mastered are opportunities won"? I'm sure there are many entrepreneurs who have fought their way successfully through the battleground of starting up a business and who smile knowingly at one of his most celebrated epigrams: "There is nothing more exhilarating than to be shot at without result."

Other than my own father, I can't think of a man for whom I've had greater admiration. But were I forced to summarize Churchill's life with a single triumph—one that has had direct impact on my life—I would say this: He helped to save freedom at a time when it was under the gravest of threats.

Creative capitalism is a potent force—arguably, the most powerful mankind has invented. But it requires a level playing field. It requires economic stability. It requires justice. More than anything, it requires freedom. I came of age in the post-war years and the world that Sir Winston Churchill saved is the one in which I have lived and worked. It is the world in which I have been fortunate enough to do business, and as I reflect now on my experiences as an entrepreneur, I find myself automatically reflecting on our debt to the subject of the portrait that hangs in a place of honour in my study. To paraphrase England's greatest prime minister, never have so many owed so much to one man.

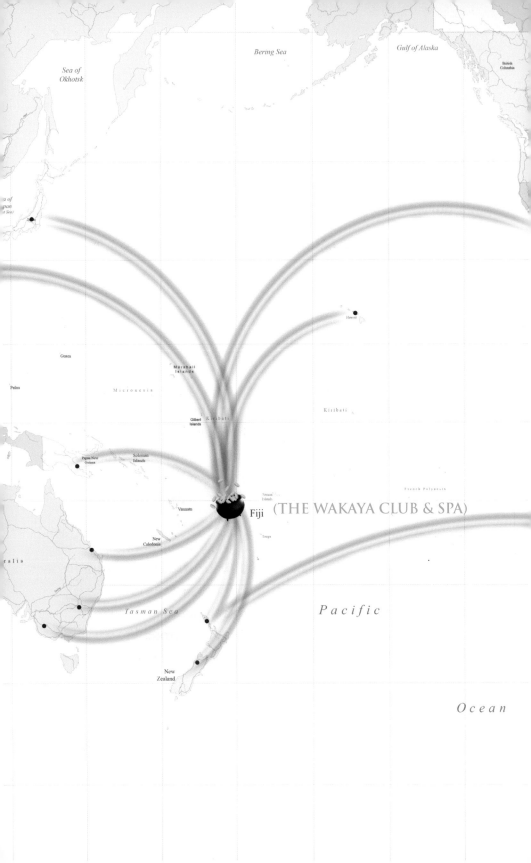

PREAMBLE AT DAWN

> *"To improve is to change. To be perfect is to change often."*
> —Sir Winston Churchill

I ALWAYS COME BACK TO WAKAYA.

It's not hard to fall in love with this island. Most visitors do. It's a 2,200-acre jewel in the Fijian chain, in the Koro Sea, less than a hundred miles to the northeast of Fiji's main airport at Nadi. I saw it for the first time in 1972, two centuries after its earliest European admirer landed—almost—on its shore.

Captain William Bligh spied its white beaches, soaring cliffs, and lush interior on May 8, 1789. After the famous *Bounty* mutiny, Bligh was set adrift in an open boat with the crewmen loyal to him. In his logbook he wrote, "As we approached Wakaya, two large sailing canoes approached. We, therefore, apprehensive that their intentions were to attack us, rowed with some anxiety, knowing that we were very weak."

Bligh was a master of understatement: The situation was more dire than his sangfroid indicates. There were seven men at sea in a single longboat. They were "with no firearms," and their supplies consisted of two coconuts. I suspect that there are entrepreneurs reading this—captains of capitalism who find themselves on the storm-tossed seas of venture and commerce— who can picture Bligh's predicament all too accurately. Anyone in the business of starting up businesses knows something about apprehension and anxiety.

My introduction to Wakaya was a little less stressful than Captain Bligh's, thankfully. Apprehension and anxiety are far removed from day-to-day life here, although I don't want to give the impression that my mind shifts into neutral when I come to Fiji. The opposite is true, actually.

Focus is fundamental to success in business. During a start-up, I like to bear down obsessively on a particular challenge or marketing strategy. My single-mindedness can push all other concerns into the background. When, for example, we were trying to come up with the perfect bottle and label for FIJI Water, the bottled water company I founded in 1997 (and sold in 2004), we went through 32 versions before we hit on the right design. As soon as I saw it, I knew it was right. But until that moment, whether I was in Fiji or in the United States, the FIJI Water label and bottle were constantly on my mind.

But sometimes, here on Wakaya, I let myself be a little less focused. I think of this as my morning preamble—a chance to follow one subject to another, to see where my thoughts and my memories and my observations will take me, to circle back on things in a meditative loop of connections that, in my mind's eye, is best represented by the ancient Egyptian symbol, the ankh.

Sega na Leqa is the name of our home on Wakaya. It is by the sea, only a short walk from our small, lovely resort, The Wakaya Club and Spa. And when I sit on the deck of Sega na Leqa, I often let my imagination roam as I watch the sky change at dawn.

When the sky changes, the sea changes. And when the sea has changed, and I pull my rapt attention back to the burnished light on the trees, I see that they have changed, too. And by then, of course, the sky has changed again. Here, every morning, I witness something everyone who is starting up a new business—or, for that matter, starting up a new chapter of their life—should accept as an absolute given: Everything is connected to what has come before and what will come after. Change is the only constant.

Wakaya has always been a magical place for me. Even the way it came into my life resonates with two things that lie very close to the core of who I am: my friendships and my businesses. My first trip to Wakaya was as a businessman assessing its possibilities. I was a young businessman, I realize now—although I didn't think so then. And my partner at the time was another young man named Peter Munk. We were close friends in those days. We still are.

The island was one of a number of properties acquired by Southern Pacific Hotels—a company I helped found in 1971 with Peter. After the roller-coaster ride of our first major business collaboration—Clairtone Sound Corporation—Southern Pacific was our next joint venture.

Curiously, the fates seemed to have already aligned my course with the distant islands of Fiji. In the early 1960s, Peter and I bought, sight unseen, a 12-acre piece of property in the South Pacific. To be clear: This was not Wakaya, nor even part of it, but our little acquisition proved to be our springboard to Southern Pacific Hotels and, for me, to the island that has become my spiritual home.

At the time, our real estate purchase in the South Pacific was very much on the periphery of our thinking. We were busy with Clairtone and it would be some years before I travelled to the South Pacific to begin putting together a plan that would become Southern Pacific Hotels.

We made that first purchase of land in the South Pacific a little cavalierly, with no grand scheme in mind. We were acting on the friendly advice of an acquaintance in Toronto who convinced us that the South Pacific had enormous potential and pointed out that the location he was suggesting had no property tax. What did we have to lose?

Not long after we acquired our first South Pacific property—and almost a decade before I made my first trip there—I found myself seated at a dinner party in Los Angeles beside the famous astrologer and psychic Jeane Dixon. Naturally, I asked her to make a prediction. We'd never met, and once she realized I wasn't interested in the Hollywood gossip that was commanding the attention of the table, she considered me carefully. She said, "You're going to play a strong role in the last pure place in the world." She thought for a moment. "I think perhaps this last safe place is … Fiji. Have you ever heard of it?"

It speaks volumes about how very far away Fiji seemed from North America and Europe in those days that Jeane's question was not had I ever been to Fiji, but rather, had I ever heard of it. Still, it was uncanny. I'm not sure who was more surprised—me, because of the specific nature of her question, or Jeane Dixon, when I said, "Actually, I have. In fact, my partner and I have just bought a small piece of land there."

Wakaya never quite worked its way effectively into Southern Pacific's portfolio, which was just as well. Soon enough, I bought the almost completely undeveloped island from my Southern Pacific partners. Somehow, I'd come to realize that it was going to be an important place for me. Business and friendship led me to Wakaya. But it always felt as if the island found me, and not the other way around.

Both entrepreneurship and friendship have been strong currents throughout my professional life. They are themes that I often consider as I sit in the early morning here on the deck of Sega na Leqa. Things have a way of coming full circle, especially if you are observant of life's cycles and patient enough to watch carefully as they turn.

Recently, the work that I have been doing with Russell Thornley, Wakaya's manager of Island Operations and Agriculture, has made me even more aware of these cycles. Our objective is to make The Wakaya Club and Spa entirely self-sustaining while leaving as little of an environmental footprint as possible—and with Russell's experience, practical skills, and devotion to the precepts of organic agriculture, we are now very close to reaching that goal. Wakaya's virgin, volcanic soil is so rich in nutrients, our environment so pristine, and the climate so generous, that we have also begun to export our organic ginger and dilo products to the world under the name of my newest start-up, Wakaya Perfection. Our ginger is the purest and most potent ginger in the world, and our dilo cream is a natural skin care product made from the seed of the dilo tree, which has extraordinarily healthful and regenerative qualities. We are also just weeks away from packaging and exporting the very finest turmeric and sea-salt on the market today – all emanating from the most perfect and purest spot on earth, Wakaya Island. Wakaya Perfection is a brand that we believe resonates with the quest of discerning consumers today for organic products of superior quality, and my belief in this quest has already been proven with Oprah Winfrey's designation of Wakaya Perfection as one of her "Favorite Things for the Holidays."

I am so proud of the very early successes that we have had with Wakaya Perfection—and know the best is yet to come! While dilo and ginger currently make up the bulk of our exports from Wakaya, new and exciting products are coming soon, including organic turmeric and organic kosher sea-salt from the pristine waters surrounding Wakaya! Nothing but the best organic products from the very best organic island on earth.

I sometimes wonder if my passion for our agricultural team's projects has also to do with the kinship I see between the natural world and the equally rewarding, equally unforgiving laws of capitalism. My father straddled these two worlds. He was a prominent businessman in Toronto and, during my teenage years, our family also owned a working farm a short distance north of the city. As a result, my roots are deep in the soil of both commerce and agriculture. Possibly the cycles to which farmers pay such close attention and the ups and downs of supply and demand hold the same fascination for me. Both seem to be systems of great complexity that are based on a process that, in its purest form, is utterly simple: Invest, nurture, raise, harvest.

Nineteenth- and twentieth-century capitalism had two areas of monumental triumph: industrial production and communications. I believe that the same potential for the creation of wealth today resides in the realm of sustainability, whether we are speaking of something as enormous and far-reaching as the digital publishing revolution or something as specific as deciding how long to leave our ginger paddocks fallow on Wakaya. Invest, nurture, raise, harvest—these remain the bedrock. But a new imperative has been added: We must be clever with our resources. The future is going to be about being smarter.

Whenever I am faced with a challenge or a problem, my instinct is always to get away from the hustle and bustle of life—to step for a moment to a view of the sky or verdant fields. This was true at Far Hills—our family farm north of Toronto. And it's true here, when I look out to the ocean from our home on the island of Wakaya. I see in the natural world an elegant balance and an uncluttered purpose that, on an infinitely smaller scale, I try to emulate in my own ventures.

During my career, I have played a role in more than ten business start-ups—which is a long list of occupations for someone who, since 1968, has had neither a salary nor (the sine qua non of corporate achievement) a company car. My journey has had its share of successes. But there were also setbacks—and while the successes have been sweet, the setbacks have also proven to be a good thing, in their way.

Uncomfortable though they are, setbacks have a way of teaching business lessons with particular clarity, and I like to think that my experiences, positive and negative, might prove helpful to a sector of the economy for which I have unbounded respect. Entrepreneurs are, by definition, individualists. They find their own way and do their own thing, which is what creating and nurturing wealth is all about. But they are not such solo-flyers that they cannot learn from the lessons taught by the triumphs and disasters of others. I don't think they need constantly to reinvent the wheel. Making mistakes that have already been made is as much of a waste of time as not paying attention to what has already succeeded. I have lessons to pass on from both sides of the ledger, which, I suppose, is the reason for this book.

Whether aspiring or battle-worn with experience, entrepreneurs are the advance-guard of free enterprise. They send out no newsletters and attend no professional conventions. Often they labour well outside the glare of the media's fickle attentions. But those who use the tools of capitalism for purposes of creation—of ideas, of products, of companies, of wealth—are one of the most valuable of America's human resources.

The approach of the entrepreneur is distinct from that of the opportunist. An opportunist is someone who, while often very clever and cunning, sees an existing idea and takes advantage of it. There are many successful business people who are opportunists, who see weaknesses in companies or false starts, and who, like sharks, smell blood in the water. They move in to take advantage of a good idea. They buy what is advantageously available, and the truth is that often they bring no added value to a project. This is a bit like graveyard dancing or ambulance chasing, but it can be a real talent, and it requires its own skills. However, as far as I am concerned, it lacks the great thrill of entrepreneurialism: the invention of something new, the creation of something that did not exist before. In this light, I often think of opportunists as being like critics. They are, as the Irish playwright Brendan Behan once said, "Like eunuchs in a harem; they know how it's done, they've seen it done every day, but they're unable to do it themselves."

Americans have developed a sophisticated proficiency as managers, bankers, traders, and investors. The contributions of these sectors to our nation's well-being (recent financial calamities and the policies of our current governments notwithstanding) should not be underestimated. But it is the creativity of the entrepreneur that is the heartbeat of our economy. It is the incentive to invent new products, establish new methods of production, and attend to new markets that is the true genius of capitalism.

I am a conservative, and chief among my reasons for disagreeing with many of the prevailing notions of the day is my conviction that over-regulation and over-taxation stand in the way of the entrepreneur. It is fashionable these days to speak of the decline of America, a conversational fad for which I have little patience. It is tempting, for example, to imagine that the decline of a great nation was evident in the tawdry spectacle of the 2011 Academy Awards, an event at which tasteless mediocrity was given tacky pride of place on the fabled red carpet. If I spend another evening watching inarticulate, unkempt, unshaven actors and uncouth actresses who look as if they have been poured into off-the-rack bridesmaid's dresses, it will be too soon. Frankly, I can't imagine worse role models for young people today.

Please don't misunderstand me. I have only respect for great actors; I've known a few. Theirs is a remarkable talent. But America's hyped-up, runaway cult of Celebrity does not reflect well on the best of them, and the more I listened to the "stars" on Oscar night, the more I was reminded of what the very great actor Sir Ralph Richardson once said: "If you have half a mind to be an actor, you have more than enough." Once elegant, once fun, the Academy Awards have become a dispiriting wallow in the shallows of celebrity.

But the decline of America? I think not, for the simple reason that behind the flashbulbs, the moronic interviews, the fawning publicists, and behind every egocentric "star," there is an army of hard-working, innovative, and intensely creative people—cinematographers, editors, sound recordists, animators, directors, designers, writers, technicians, and computer wizards whose work is what makes American movies the most potent force of popular culture in the world.

Similarly, I don't see much "decline" in the explosion of e-readers and electronic tablets that are revolutionizing the publishing industry.

I believe that the spirit of innovation, whether in moviemaking or in more conventional businesses, is America's great strength. Start-ups are the bellwether of our economy, and we place obstruction and restriction in the way of the entrepreneur at our peril. Most politicians and bureaucrats see things differently, of course—a point of view that may have a great deal to do with the fact that they are more accustomed to cashing their pay cheques and filing for expense claims than paying salaries to employees. My experience is that the people most intent on the redistribution of wealth are the ones who, endlessly apologizing for the success of others, have never created it themselves.

In times of economic uncertainty, new business ventures are even more important than in periods of calm and stability. Now more than ever, we should be doing whatever we can to encourage the entrepreneurial spirit on which this nation is founded, and not stifling it by naïve policy, however well-intentioned. We may not yet be in danger of waking up and finding ourselves in a socialist state. But we are distracted by silliness. We are dazzled by the trite and inconsequential. We are suffering under the illusion that we can overcome fear with regulation and minimize risk with legislated obstruction. Worst of all, we sometimes lose sight of the power of creativity. We are coming closer and closer to extinguishing the spark of imagination that lights the fire of possibility.

When I was 20, it must have looked, from my father's vantage point, that there was not much direction to my life. And lack of direction was extremely worrisome to his generation. The Depression was not a distant memory. He knew that it was possible, both for economies and for individuals, to go very wrong. Dad's military and business background led him to believe that venturing from the straight and narrow would not be a wise course. He believed that I would find fulfillment as a broker or in an investment house—that, in other words, I should get a job.

I knew that wasn't for me. I didn't like to pursue a path that ran counter to Dad's wishes. But I just couldn't see myself in an office, and not because I felt above such things. I've always enjoyed the camaraderie of working with others. Today, I work with old and new friends alike, and look forward to my times with them and all members of my various teams. I always leave inspired and excited by our many prospects and ambitions. The office environment my father had in mind—the kind of office environment that prevailed in Toronto in the 1950s—was not quite so exhilarating.

Even as a young man, I knew that office routine would stifle any strengths that I have. I knew I wouldn't be happy following in my father's footsteps, particularly in a city as relatively insular as Toronto was at that time. My father was a well-known figure on Bay Street (Canada's version of Wall Street), and I knew that in certain Toronto circles I would always be Harrison Gilmour's son. Perhaps striking out on my own was just a matter of pride.

Whatever the motivation, I embarked down a road that must have looked fraught with peril to my father. And I suppose it was.

One of the curiosities of my life is that even though Dad would probably have advised against my becoming an independent entrepreneur, and even though, sadly, he died before I realized my early success, it is his general wisdom that has been one of the guiding lights of my career.

Dad was often extremely canny in response to suggestions I presented to him when I was young—suggestions that, more obviously than I imagined, served some purpose of my own. Once, for example, when I was travelling alone in Europe for the first time, I was running out of money but by no means anxious to end my European adventure. I sent word, by what in those days was called the night letter, to my father. I told him that I had been travelling so much that the tires on my little Volkswagen were now bald, and I needed $300 for a new set. His reply was not exactly chatty, but his quiet sense of humor was apparent. He'd seen through my ruse, but he didn't really blame me for trying. "Pull vehicle to side of road. Abandon. Your safety our paramount concern. Return home."

As I get older my father only grows in my esteem. He handled himself with a calm sense of what was and what was not important, and the advice he gave had a way of turning into beliefs I hold to this day.

I remember that before my European travels, when I was only 16 years old and home in Toronto on a midterm break from the boarding school I was attending, Dad asked me to have a word with him in his study. I recall perching nervously on the left end of the large sofa in his study. He was sitting in his wingback chair. Our family was comfortably off, but Dad made it clear that no vast trust fund would be coming my way. Under discussion was whether I'd like him to put aside something for seed money for a future business, or whether I'd prefer to spend the same amount travelling.

This was by no means a lopsided question. Dad could see that there were good reasons to choose either option, so long as the choice was made thoughtfully and with conviction. He may have had doubts about an uncertain path, but he had none about what success requires. "You can do anything you set about to do," he said, "if you do it honestly, and if you work hard. Self-doubt undermines confidence, and without confidence, any project suffers, if not fails." That advice is as useful to me today as it was 60 years ago.

Later in life I learned another valuable and relevant lesson from and about my father—that he had received the Military Cross and Bar by helping save his comrades trapped by barbed wire in "no man's land" during a fierce battle during WWI. My father ventured out on several occasions to retrieve his injured comrades in his underwear to avoid the often lethal bacterial infections that occured when soldiers were shot or wounded while wearing full battle dress. Again my father proved that action is what matters—whether in the trenches of 1917 or in the meeting rooms of 2013.

I am not particularly well known as a businessman. My relative anonymity runs contrary to contemporary society's mania for celebrity and penchant for self-promotion. But that's fine by me. "The spouting whale gets the harpoon" is an old saying of my father's that I have taken very much to heart. I have never yearned very much for attention—not enough, certainly, to make it a goal. Even as a younger businessman, I was content to let my partner and friend, Peter Munk, take centre stage—because that was my nature and that was the nature of our partnership. Peter's irrepressible enthusiasm made him very good at being in the spotlight.

To the extent that I have a public profile today, it is probably as the founder of FIJI Water, although my more recent venture of Wakaya Perfection is beginning to make it difficult for me to stay entirely in the shadows. As has happened from time to time in my life, the press has been calling.

Turns out that I have ended up at the centre of a revolution in human culture, the dimensions of which are staggering.

Zinio.com, a thriving young company of which I am the majority owner, is the world's largest global, digital newsstand, distributing more than 5,000 magazine titles, books, catalogues, and newsletters in digital form to more than 190 countries. (Cuba and Venezuela are currently the exceptions, but I am confident that one day soon that too shall change.) Zinio is now one of the premier reading applications for the many e-readers and electronic tablets that are fueling a red-hot market. We are ubiquitous. Zinio delivers globally, operating in 19 currencies and 33 languages, and its custom publishing division is setting new industry standards. It is, in my view, at the very leading edge of the new reading revolution. By way of demonstrating how much the world has changed, I like to point out that, through Zinio, I get the new issue of *The Economist* on my island in Fiji the day before my friends, Lynn and Sir Evelyn Rothschild, who are major shareholders of *The Economist*, get theirs in London.

Timing is everything, and throughout my career of start-ups I seem to have had a knack for it. But never more so than now. I have ventured into publishing at the very dawn of a new golden age of publishing.

FIJI Water sticks in people's minds. It astonishes me that long after we sold the company that I started in 1996, a lightbulb often seems to go on when anyone is told that I'm "the guy who started FIJI Water." It makes me think we got it right.

It is a source of great satisfaction to know that the marketing strategy that I created has proven to be so successful. Especially so because our tactics were born of necessity. Ingenuity was the only tool we had.

We knew we couldn't come close to matching the advertising budgets of our biggest competitors, and so we were obliged to use our imaginations. We couldn't afford to take the conventional path. So we found an unconventional one. We approached the marketing of FIJI Water with the same absence of orthodoxy that went into the product's conception.

To this day, people are intrigued by the story. How, in a field with 620 direct competitors and dominated by the soft drink and bottled-water giants, we accomplished the difficult task of establishing a national brand within five years of product launch. Our plan followed a strategy that is my marketing mantra: visibility, trial, advocacy. We made the product visible and, by virtue of its visibility, people tried it, and then because the product either fulfilled or exceeded their expectations, they became advocates on its behalf. That simple paradigm continues to work its magic, and is almost always the template for any future marketing plans that I contemplate.

I am pleased to be introduced as "the guy who started FIJI Water." Pleased because it is a superior product with many healthful benefits, and pleased because we figured out how to make our customers and potential customers understand that to be true. In the context of the industry into which I stepped, a campaign to build a national brand was almost certain to be a long, expensive, painstaking process. We had come from out of the blue, and yet, in marketing terms, FIJI Water became recognizable in the blink of an eye. FIJI Water seemed to be in the hands, always, of the most sought-after celebrities at the most fashionable parties and galas. Suddenly, and not by accident, it was in scenes in television shows and movies when the director wanted to signal to the viewer that "classiness" was on display. Store owners placed it prominently because it was one of those products that made a store look better for carrying it. Just a glance at the distinctive turquoise of the original design on our bottles (a design its new owners have changed) registered name recognition. To this day, there are restaurants that serve no bottled water other than FIJI Water. I'm proud of all that. But I'm also very proud of the fact that there are business schools that use the FIJI Water story as a case study in marketing. Visibility creates trial, which creates advocacy. A business rule to live by. I certainly have.

If anyone is familiar with my history beyond FIJI Water, they tend to link my name with that of my longtime friend and former partner Peter Munk, the Chairman of Barrick Gold. While Peter and I have been involved in four major start-ups together, my years as an entrepreneur didn't begin with my association with him. But I wasn't very far out of the starting gate when we met, and my career certainly picked up speed after we joined forces.

Our first venture together was Clairtone Sound Corporation Limited—a Canadian hi-fi manufacturer that began brilliantly in the late 1950s and ended badly in the early 1970s.

Remarkably enough, Peter and I survived with our partnership and, more remarkably still, our friendship intact. My affection and respect for Peter only grow as the years pass.

The demise of Clairtone was not a pretty picture—a lesson about the dangers of mixing up business ventures with governments that neither Peter nor I have ever forgotten. My concerns about government, labour unions, and over-regulation may not have had their origins in the Clairtone debacle, but they certainly came of age with it.

Clairtone was all about innovation, originality and treading on virgin sands in the face of great headwinds. It was about the latest components and startling, fresh design. It was all about being new, which, I think, is the very essence of entrepreneurship. But through a combination of ambition and naïvety, Peter and I formed alliances with forces that proved to be entirely opposed to the entrepreneurial spirit. We were shocked by the experience of watching our dream trampled by the anticorporate agendas of unions and elected officials. This was an important lesson to learn, our Ph.D. in the school of hard knocks. But fortunately, for us, it was something we experienced when we were young and resilient and able to bounce back. Not everyone is so lucky, and there are so many examples of setbacks that have been fatal to ventures and to careers.

Almost immediately, we started wondering what to do next. Quickly enough we became engaged in one of the many long, ongoing conversations that have animated both our partnerships and our friendship throughout our professional lives. Peter and I talked, and talked, and talked—and as we did, an idea began to take shape.

This, I believe, is a characteristic of the true entrepreneur: the ability to begin. And to begin again. And again. An absolute requirement of the job is the ability to get up and start over with renewed vigor and increased wisdom after a setback. Because there will be setbacks. That I can guarantee. As is so often the case, Winston Churchill put it best: "Success consists of going from failure to failure without loss of enthusiasm."

One of man's greatest weaknesses is to blame others for failures, weaknesses, and shortcomings. That is why the search for someone to blame is always successful. My two favourite quotations on this subject are as follows: "The keenest sorrow is to recognize ourselves as the sole cause of all our adversities." (Sophocles.) And, "When you blame others, you give up your power to change." (Douglas Adams.)

Peter and I often remark that had Clairtone continued from success to success, we might have ended up as comfortably well-off hi-fi manufacturers—which wouldn't have been half as much fun or rewarding as the many adventures for both of us that followed Clairtone's demise. I'm inclined to think that there are reasons for things unfolding as they do. As the saying goes, "It's darkest before the dawn." And nobody knows the meaning of that old chestnut better than an entrepreneur.

Peter and I got on with things as a result of a pretty

straightforward inspiration: the practical matter of our survival. After Clairtone, neither of us could afford to take the time to do much wound-licking.

Neither of us had inherited wealth. As young men we were both restless and ambitious. So we did what we would do several times in our careers: We ignored most of the cautionary advice we were getting.

We turned our energies to the vast potential of resort and hotel real estate in the Pacific Rim. And our thinking—as the best thinking often is—was simple. We had figured out that while a growing market was there, the big hotel chains of Europe and North America were not. We wouldn't have to take on any sharks in what was then, commercially speaking, a small pond.

Southern Pacific acquired and developed many properties—hotels, resorts, a golf course. Wakaya was one of our assets, but the company never quite figured out what to do with the beautiful little island, which was a lucky break for me. I was beginning to have some ideas for it, myself.

I've travelled a good deal (more than eight million miles); I've had more addresses than I care to count. But I have never felt anything for a place like what I feel for Wakaya, our island paradise in Fiji. I had an immediate connection with the white beaches and soaring bluffs that Captain Bligh had so hopefully spotted on the horizon. As time has passed, my bond has only grown stronger. My daughter Erin—my only child—and I holidayed often on Wakaya.

I bought the island from my business partners a few years after my first visit there in 1972. I was acting on a hunch—a premonition, I suppose—that it would become an important place to me.

And so it has. The most important place I know, as a matter of fact. It's home, and one of the reasons I have chosen it for that role is because I can do something to return what it has given me. I can preserve its beauty. There aren't many places that grant us that possibility.

So many other places that have been dear to me—St. Tropez, Majorca, Marbella, Acapulco, Puerto Vallarta, and Hawaii, to name but a few—have, in my view, been ruined as compared with their original beauty. Mass tourism is to culture what an oil spill is to ecology. But Wakaya gave me a unique opportunity to find a home and, at the same time, protect it. The island had been virtually uninhabited since 1838, and therefore offered me a chance to create a new beginning for one of the most beautiful places I know.

Our home is part of a small resort that has been created by me and, more importantly, by my wife, Jill. Our ambition at The Wakaya Club and Spa is the creation of something truly, lastingly beautiful—something that will have a truly impactful effect on visitors who come here to unwind, to refresh, or perhaps even to find themselves. The Wakaya Club and Spa is a retreat that is as close to perfection as we can get. But perfection isn't perfection at all if its future is not secure. I've learned that lesson well enough in my life.

And so our home on Wakaya and The Wakaya Club and Spa is about the preservation of extraordinary beauty. Jill and I have established a rigorous conservation plan, one that will continue in perpetuity. This is fundamentally important, for the simple reason that Wakaya is so valued by us both. My former partners have sometimes kidded me about my purchase of the island. I paid for it with stock that quadrupled not long after I'd traded it to them for a property that they didn't know what to do with, but I have never felt the slightest pang of regret.

The island of Wakaya is about 20 minutes by air from Fiji's capital, Suva. As our (happily-arriving, sadly-departing) guests know, Wakaya is only about a 40-minute flight from the international airport at Nadi in the resort's private Cessna Grand Caravan, or as I like to refer to it, our flying luxury limousine.

But Wakaya feels a long way away from everywhere, even other islands of Fiji. Even during an abrupt change of administration, Fijian politics are as distant to our guests as Suva's traffic. Indeed, what is going on in the capital often has more resonance in much more distant points than on Wakaya, in large part because agencies such as the U.S. State Department and the international press can be counted on to make things sound considerably more alarming than they actually are.

Once, not so many years ago, the well-known actor Patrick Stewart and his fiancée were booked to come to The Wakaya Club and Spa for their honeymoon. As a result of the

State Department's knee-jerk reaction to a "coup" (one of the five virtually bloodless government takeovers that I have experienced during my years in Fiji), a travel warning was issued to American citizens shortly before the newlyweds' departure from Los Angeles.

Stewart called Gavin de Becker, exactly the right person to consult. De Becker's 250-member firm, Gavin de Becker & Associates, provides security for high-level government officials, business executives, and celebrities. An advisor to the Rand Corporation, de Becker also happens to own a beautiful piece of property in Fiji. Stewart had been a client. Few people know more about international security than de Becker, and almost nobody combines this knowledge with an intimate association with Fiji. Who better to turn to for advice?

De Becker listened patiently to Stewart's concerns, and his reply rings in my mind to this day. It demonstrated eminent common sense—common sense that I wish the State Department could have in greater abundance. "Patrick," de Becker said, "the dangerous part of your trip will be between your house in Los Angeles and the Los Angeles airport. Not in Fiji." As a result of this advice, Stewart and his beautiful bride came to Wakaya. They had a happy, relaxed, untroubled stay.

During the 40 years that I have been coming to Fiji—a period that coincides almost precisely with Fiji's independence after 96 years of British colonial rule—the nation's growing pains have certainly been evident at times. But time and again, the leaders of Fiji have proven that plunder is not their motivation for power. For the most part, they have been intent on improving the conditions of life in their nation each in their own way, and the global tourist is still both loved and respected by all Fijians as he or she has been for so long.

In 2006, when Fiji's military commander took over the elected parliamentary government, friends of ours from the United States and Europe e-mailed or phoned in great consternation. A coup! They wanted to know how we were doing: I think they pictured us huddled around a radio with artillery rumbling in the distance and supplies running low.

"Well," I replied, "our guests are snorkeling, and going on picnics, and sitting on the chaises in front of their *bures* reading, or sunning, or looking out to the magnificent view. The ones who are good tennis players are meeting their friends, the good golfers, on the level playing field of our professional croquet court. I can almost hear the quiet thunk of the mallets David Niven gave to Jill and me. I can see a school of dolphin passing from where I am standing. The weather is perfect. The lunch today was divine. I'm having a massage this afternoon. We are doing quite well, thank you. How are you doing?"

Dumbfounded silence was generally the response to my reporting from "the front."

I don't mean to be naïve about the roughshod ways of military dictatorships. Both my father and my grandfather fought for democracy, so its overthrow anywhere is not something I take lightly. But I have to say, the debates in America about healthcare, or in the U.K. about spending cutbacks, or in Canada about Quebec secession are generally more heated than any of the Fijian "coups" I have experienced. Modern, independent Fiji is a country that is less than 50 years old, and yet I have never seen anything in its internal politics that can compare with the divisiveness that is currently the hallmark of the U.S. House and Senate—institutions of a republic that has had almost two and a half centuries to get its legislative act together.

In my experience, Fijian "coups" have been more civilized than the hurled spittoons and duels that characterized an average day in the House of Representatives for many years after American independence. (I'm convinced that the only reason spittoons are no longer used as missiles in Congress is because, with tobacco chewing out of fashion, they are no longer fixtures of the chambers.) In any case, I see no decline in the partisan fury that so frequently sent them flying in the first place. And were duels still regarded as an acceptable way to settle political scores and avenge personal insult, I'm sure that pistols-at-dawn would be as common in Washington today as they were when Dolley Madison was First Lady and Abraham Lincoln was a toddler.

If America is more civilized in its political discourse than it used to be, the improvement cannot be said to be vast. Never, for instance, have I heard a Fijian leader refer to his opposition as "the enemy," a term that the President of the United States recently used to describe Republicans opposed to his policies.

But one ignores politics at one's peril. A quick glance at the history of the years before the Second World War makes that point with graphic clarity, and my father was someone who read the ominous signs clearly. I am not recommending heads in the sand. One cannot be an admirer of Winston Churchill and think that doing nothing in the face of a gathering storm is an acceptable course of action.

I am merely suggesting a reality check, not something the State Department seems to encourage when it comes to Fiji. I am merely recommending knowledge—again, not always the State Department's strong suit. Its reading of the situation in Fiji has been almost as accurate as its reading of the situation in North Africa and the Middle East—and that was an explosion that State somehow didn't see coming until it was on the television news.

As someone who is very active in Fiji's economic life and who concerns himself with the general welfare of the Fijian people, I make it my business to keep my ear to the ground about goings-on in the nation's capital. I make it my business to be informed. This has not always been Washington's strategy. During the Clinton administration, when the wife of the American ambassador to Fiji decided that she missed her grandchildren and the couple returned to the U.S., their abandoned diplomatic post was left vacant for two years! Not much of an ear, and not anywhere close to the ground. I sometimes wonder whether we would be a little less quick with travel restrictions—and whether an ambassadorship would be left vacant for two years—if pools of oil and not aquifers of water were under Fijian soil.

I don't become involved in factional politics, and so long as administrations are working toward improving the lot of Fijians, I see no reason for an outsider to interfere. My interests are in building new industries in Fiji, in creating exports, and by creating exports, helping to align the balance of payments. My chief priorities are Wakaya Island, The Wakaya Club and Spa, and Wakaya Perfection, along with the building of preschools throughout Fiji—schools that will teach children the all important lessons of how to learn in preparation for their entrance into elementary school. Every Fijian administration has been supportive of these goals.

I take a long view—a position that, in the ebb and flow of politics, has proven to be wise. I've been doing business in Fiji for 40 years. I am whatever the opposite of a carpetbagger is. I am friendly with Fijian accountants, Fijian lawyers, Fijian business people, and Fijian citizens from all walks of life. I take the time to ask them and to ask the Fijians in our employ what their views are. And if they are reasonably content with the efforts of an administration, I think it would be presumptuous of me to pretend I know better.

I confess to some impatience when my American, Australian, and New Zealand friends react with total alarm to Fiji's internal struggles. What, after all, was America like a few decades after independence? Not exactly an oasis of political and social calm.

As it so happens, my own family history has a strong connection with exactly this tumult. Not very many generations back, we were, on my father's side, members of that group of refugees from America known as United Empire Loyalists.

My family, having left first Scotland and then Northern Ireland in search of opportunity, was granted property in Vermont by the British Crown. During the time of the Revolutionary War, it was entirely plausible that, were the rebels successful, my family's land would have been confiscated.

Such uncertainty is almost impossible for us to imagine today. My ancestors were not rabid supporters of the British Crown. They were plain, God-fearing Protestants, anxious about their family and their property. As a result, they did what refugees in North Africa, in the Middle East, in Asia, do to this day: They headed for the borders. They left for British North America. They ended up in Canada. When I think about my family's history and about Jeane Dixon's prediction for me, I wonder if the ability to look forward and see trouble on the horizon and to then act accordingly might be an innate survival skill that some have and some, sadly, do not. There are always people who wait too long to act.

Wakaya is where I am sitting now, looking out over the curls of surf breaking on the distant coral reefs. The view from the deck of our house is of Homestead Bay, the safest and most beautiful anchorage in the South Pacific. It's a vista that is a kind of meditation for me. I like to take it in. I like to be observant of its details.

The best commercial ideas of my career have come to me on Wakaya while daydreaming, reading, or exploring the vistas that unfold before my eyes every minute of every day. As hunches go, Wakaya was one of my better ones.

I live by hunches, but not by wild guesses. They are different beasts, and the distinction is an important one. Good hunches, in my experience, are never shots in the dark. They are actually predictions that are informed by watchfulness and by experience.

Throughout history, there have been events that have caused major changes in human behavior. We are going through such a period now, the transition from decades of fiscal profligacy and unnecessary waste to what *The New York Times* columnist Thomas Friedman predicts is the emergence of the "Re-Generation." And I hope that Friedman is right. Certainly, the possibilities opened up by the revolution of computers and digital communication make that seem much more than wishful thinking. In my view, the recalibration is a necessity. We are at a point where we have to use the spark of change to kindle the flame of creative, sustainable capitalism.

The shifts and realignments of history can be grand historic revolutions and cataclysms, or they can be realignments of commerce and markets. Or, more commonly, they can be combinations of both.

Buying habits as well as design and style preferences are impacted by shifts large and small, and the successful entrepreneur is someone who can recognize these trends before others do. The ability to recognize a style, a desire, or a fashion before it exists in the popular imagination is not something for which anyone gets a degree. So we describe these prognostications with understatement of which even Captain Bligh would have approved. We call them hunches.

The present is difficult enough to see clearly, let alone the future. The trees have a habit of getting in the way of the forest. But with the benefit of hindsight (one of the few things that I have more of, the older I get), I can see that my career as an entrepreneur has been all about hunches. It's been all about trying to see signs in the present that point to changes yet to come. Let me give you an example.

Immediately after the Second World War, the longing for brightness, for cleverness, for simplicity, for innovation, and for casual elegance was very strong—even if most of Europe was too devastated to acknowledge this. Fashion couldn't be much more than a daydream for people who had to struggle to survive. I saw the aftermath of the war with my own eyes in 1948 when, as a young traveller, I stepped off trains and saw the flattened ruins of once-proud cities stretch before me. For many, the very basics of food, shelter, and safety were more of a priority than design. But humans are humans—drawn to beauty and appreciative of its luster—and a longing for brightness was a natural response to the sadness, the restrictions, and the prevailing gloom of the war years.

My early European travels also took me to Scandinavia. And there, in Finland, Denmark, Sweden, and Norway, I caught a glimpse of what, compared to the spectral ruins of Hamburg, Cologne, and Dresden, seemed a ray of sunshine. As a young man I wasn't drawn to matters of domestic design or housewares. I knew a salad bowl from a soup tureen, but my knowledge didn't extend much beyond. Still, it was in this unexpected realm that the contrast to the pervasive grey of the post-war years caught my eye. My trip to Scandinavia was to visit my sister, Shelagh. She had met a Norwegian flyer when he was training in Toronto during the Second World War. (Shelagh herself volunteered to join the Norwegian Airforce and served in London during the Blitz as a radio operator while her husband was flying bombing missions on the continent.) After the war, they moved to Oslo, where during a trip to the mountains, in one of those stranger-than-fiction moments, Shelagh's husband's friend was shot in the leg by a recluse German soldier who did not know that the war was over.

In the Oslo shops, restaurants, and people's homes, I got my first sight of what we now know as Scandinavian design. I felt instinctively that this was a key to the future.

My first real commercial ventures were companies called ScanTrade and Dansk Design—companies that were, essentially, predictions that the ray of sunshine that I had seen during my travels in Scandinavia would soon break out over Europe and North America. This is exactly what happened, and this successful prediction—this hunch—reinforced my belief in the art of paying attention.

My approach to business opportunity then, as is my approach today, isn't so much thinking "outside the box." It would be more accurately described as looking closely at what's in the box for clues about what the future holds. All the major start-ups in which I have been involved—ScanTrade and Dansk Design, Clairtone, Southern Pacific, Barrick Gold, Thumper, Horsham,

TrizecHahn, The Wakaya Club and Spa, FIJI Water, *VIV*, Zinio, and Wakaya Perfection—have drawn on this skill. You can call it tea-leaf reading if you want. I call it being observant.

It was my father—a decorated war hero, a well-known Toronto merchant banker, and a great sportsman—who taught me to keep my eyes open. When I was a teenager in the late 1940s, and I decided that I would accept his offer of money to travel, he gave me the minimum of necessary funds for $10-a-day travel in Europe—but with one stipulation. He insisted that I travel alone.

This directive must seem strange to parents today. They often don't allow their children to walk home from school, let alone advise them to go to Europe, on their own. But I grew up in a different, and I sometimes think, saner era.

My father knew that if I went to Europe with my pals, I'd have a roaring, good old time. But I wouldn't meet anyone new, I wouldn't learn anything new. Likely I wouldn't see very far beyond whatever watering-hole my chums and I chose to set up camp in. So off I went to Paris, entirely on my own, and among the many things I learned from my adventures was the lesson of observing.

My father's instruction has stayed with me all my life. I have logged more than eight million miles of world travel—and that exposure to new lands and new people has proven to be an education in itself. (Any young person who asks about the wisdom of a "gap" year gets a three-word answer from me: Travel, travel, travel.) And while the great pleasures and benefits of going on journeys with friends or with a loved one are not to be denied, such excursions don't often inspire the unfettered thinking that is shared by the lone traveller and the entrepreneur. They learn to be observant; they learn that what can be learned by paying attention to character, style, motivation, habit, and desires is often critical information. They also learn a lesson that is retaught so many times in life (and one that I have recently come to appreciate even more) – and that is to trust but verify!!

I've often found being alone to be rewarding, calming, and productive. Our MBA-driven penchant for meetings and committees, and our preoccupation with "reporting reports to the reported so that they can report what's being reported" runs counter to what inventors and creators and innovators almost always say about the source of their inspiration. Whether they are philosophers or entrepreneurs, their ideas almost always come to them in solitude. It's when people are alone that the lightbulb of creativity goes on.

The field of creative capitalism is a constantly changing landscape of observation and reaction, imagination and invention, ambitious dreams and practical application. Because there are so few set rules, it is an endeavour that also involves no small amount of luck. It would be much less fun if it didn't. But the thing to remember about luck is there are two kinds: the sheer, dumb, bolt-from-the-blue kind (by which people win lotteries, or inherit millions from unknown relatives, or strike oil while digging a fence post). Then there is the luck that is altogether more useful to the entrepreneur: Luck is where preparation meets opportunity. In this very particular way, FIJI Water, Zinio, and now Wakaya Perfection have all been very lucky indeed.

But let me be more specific. As the subtitle of this book suggests, I believe that it is the job of the entrepreneur to create the products and trends of the future, not just predict them. And I believe and have significant proof positive in all I have created, that the products of the future will be all about effectiveness, sustainability, quality, and purity. Let me deconstruct: The days of the disposable product are coming to an end (thankfully,) and will be supplanted by products that stand the test of time. I entreat the entrepreneurs of the future to heed this warning— either be ready for this trend by creating those products that will last or be ready to go out of business. The trend is unmistakable, of that I am sure … as sure as I have been about Clairtone, FIJI Water and Wakaya. The consumer of the future will demand that her products be made to stand the test of time and be crafted with integrity—just as we have endeavored to do with everything related to Wakaya for over 40 years.

As I sit here on the deck of our home on Wakaya, early in the morning, tallying my lessons learned during a lifetime of business ventures, my lists seem to grow, story by story. Chapter by chapter, you might say.

The sun is just rising on the horizon, a golden sphere that morphs into a raging red fireball. The distant islands are dusty purple.

Every day, this is the first dawn in the world. The first

sound I hear when I settle into my chaise is the low continuo of waves hitting the coral reefs. It's an overture that heralds the emerging colours of turquoise and apple-jade. The surface of the sea is the colour of lapis lazuli, and the foam of surf breaking on coral reefs is the white of rock crystal. A pod of whales, perhaps as many as a hundred, passes beyond the reef on their migration south, followed by playful dolphins, wahoo, walu, black marlin, and many varieties of tuna. Flocks of seabirds dart, weave, and dive.

On shore a glorious symphony has begun, created by the 36 species of birds native to Wakaya singing their hearts out, a cappella. The performance begins with the barking pigeons, communicating with each other across the bay that a new day has dawned and all is well. The lorikeets, a variety of parrot, swoop in, hitting a chorus of piercing high C's, advising each other that a newly discovered mango tree is where they shall gather for breakfast. And then the conductor's baton of this musical extravaganza falls dramatically: A peregrine falcon, the world's fastest predator, descends hundreds of feet at 140 mph in a plummeting instant for his repast, a decent that ends in an explotion of feathers! The peregrine is one of the few birds that captures its prey in mid-flight, and its target is usually an unlucky pigeon or dove.

Songbirds add to all this, creating a glorious cacophony of sound. At the same time, the nocturnal members of the community—fallow deer and wild pigs—retreat into the tropical highlands. Feral horses groom the hillside palm groves.

Some people have asked if it isn't difficult for me to

concentrate on matters commercial in a setting of such breath-taking natural beauty. But this is exactly what ignites my imagination. This ever-changing view is the catalyst for my ideas, and the best are those that I find outside the bounds of conventional wisdom. I don't know any place better for thinking imaginatively.

And it's not just me. We have a number of Wakaya returnees who have had life-changing, wealth-creating epiphanies at The Wakaya Club and Spa. Like me, they seem able to find the missing piece of the puzzle here. Like me, they are able to put things—whether personal or business-related—into a new perspective. And finding a new perspective is, in essence, what entrepreneurs do.

There is no doubt that I am in better shape than I would otherwise be as a result of my regular stays at Wakaya. But there's more to this place than physical rejuvenation. I noticed from the first time I stepped on the island that somehow my mental faculties are also more acute. A professor from the University of Graz in Austria once told me that Wakaya is on the same biomagnetic grid as the spiritual healing centers of Lourdes and Fatima. Whether this explains the island's remarkable qualities, and whether it explains the remarkable properties of FIJI Water and our Wakaya Perfection products, is beyond my expertise, but I don't doubt the possibility. Wakaya truly is a special place, one where my energies and imagination are aligned in a way they are nowhere else. As a result, I come here two or three times a year to recharge my batteries.

If I had to choose one piece of advice for someone dreaming of starting a business, it would be what my father taught me: "The definition of wisdom is to listen when you would rather be talking." Churchill said much the same: "Courage is what it takes to stand up and speak; courage is also what it takes to sit down and listen." Whether you are planning a business, creating a product, assessing your trust level with potential partners or investors, hiring a manager or staff, or even if you are thinking about buying an island in the South Pacific, my advice is to watch, listen, and then trust your instincts. And don't underestimate the power of the hunch. Remember, Thomas Edison had a hunch about lightbulbs. So did Bill Gates, about personal computers.

Hunches are unplanned thoughts—ones that, almost by their nature, catch one unexpectedly. The idea for FIJI Water, for example, came to me on the golf course on Wakaya when I watched a player pull a bottle of Evian from a golf bag. This was something I'd seen dozens of times before, but for some reason, that day, I found it striking. Literally so. The thought hit me like a lightning bolt. Why are we drinking water from Europe—densely populated, polluted Europe—in the pristine beauty of the South Pacific? And from that simple observation sprang FIJI Water.

As a result of my habit of having ideas at unpredictable moments, I've always made notes to myself. When, as a young man, I travelled through Europe, I kept journals. At the time, like so many young Americans-in-Paris who could be found lounging in the cafés of the Boulevard Saint-Germain, I imagined that I might write a novel. For one thing, I knew I would never lack for colourful characters: I've always had a knack for running into and befriending the most interesting people. When I met Ernest Hemingway in a tapas bar in Madrid in 1951, and ended up attending a few bullfights in his company, the ambition to write a novel became even more compelling.

Alas, the novel was never written although I had many hundreds of pages done. (In fact the whole first edition of my manuscript was stolen off a platform in Victoria Station in London as I was on my way to Wales!) But I often think I've lived the novel in its entirety. I often think I am living one still—a novel recorded in what I've jotted down along the way. Files, pages, journals, diaries—the notes I've compiled in my life—would be stacked as high as my desk. Winston Churchill's pithy aphorisms, characteristic displays of wit, and expressions of wisdom run throughout all my notes to myself. Rare is the predicament on which Churchill cannot cast some welcome light. But the many chapters of this living novel of mine owe their greatest debt to my father's stipulation that I travel alone.

Had I not been alone, by way of one example, I wouldn't have struck up a friendship with the heir to one of the world's great breweries on the terrace of the Carlton Hotel in Cannes on the Riviera during my youthful travels. In 1951, Freddy Heineken saw me sitting by myself, nursing a beer—one that probably cost a significant percentage of the money in my wallet at the time. He called me over to his table, and suddenly, there I was, a young traveller, footloose and fancy-free, being introduced to the likes of Rita Hayworth and The Aga Khan. One minute, I had been watching passersby on La Croisette as all tourists do;

the next I was in the roped-off area at the Palm Beach Casino watching King Farouk sneer over his pile of million-franc chips at the baccarat table. A crowd had gathered to watch the spectacle of an ad hoc syndicate of ten young Englishmen who, with some considerable panache, were intent on taking down the King of Egypt. And who, with more panache still, succeeded.

Had I not been open to meeting people, I might never have come to know the fascinating characters who, some in passing, some in more long-term ways, have populated the story of my life: Freddy Heineken, Errol Flynn, Grace Kelly, David Niven, and good old Papa Hemingway. Hemingway's passion for the blood and sand of the bullring is still with me. His lessons have lasted far longer than what is so often the hollow thrill of meeting a celebrity. Thanks to Hemingway, I often have travelled to Spain for the express purpose of seeing a particular matador.

The novel I've lived has taken me from my birth in a town on the Canadian prairies to my upbringing in what was then sleepy, provincial Toronto. From there, the plot has unfolded in New York, London, Paris, Cairo, Sydney, Nassau, Aspen, Los Angeles, Hong Kong, Tokyo, Palm Beach, and Fiji. It is a story with chapters on businesses in which I have been involved, from my earliest ventures with ScanTrade and Dansk Design to my most recent adventures, nearly 60 years later, in the world of digital publishing and the creation of Wakaya Perfection.

It's a long way from the prairies of the pre-television age to sitting on our deck on Wakaya and dreaming of the untold possibilities of the breaking wave of the digital revolution. But all along the way I never lost the habit of jotting down notes, clipping stories, underlining passages in books (a barbaric habit, of which I do solemnly repent), and keeping track of quotes and pieces of wisdom that seem to have particular relevance to what I'm doing or to what I am about to do. Were you to go through my papers, you'd find these nuggets jotted down in notepads, pocketbooks, on scraps of paper, on the backs of envelopes. My idiosyncratic filing system does not mean these aphorisms are not important to me. Quite the contrary. In many cases, I've lived by them. And this book gives me the chance to collect them all in one place.

Buying an island in Fiji seems at a far remove from jotting down a quote in a notebook, but I see them both as part of the same process. In the case of the quotations, they are thoughts, or ideas, or distillations of philosophies that resonate with me. My instinct is to write them down for future reference. I have a sense—a hunch, an intuition—that I will need to call on them. For example, when I first jotted down the famous quotation of Winston Churchill's—"When you are going through hell, keep going"—I had no idea how directly those words would apply to a dark and difficult passage I was required to go through in my own life. There were days when I clung to the wisdom of those words as if to a life raft.

Similarly, I'm not sure that when I first conceived of buying the island of Wakaya I could have articulated exactly what my reasons were. Somehow, though, I knew I was acquiring it because I would need it in the future. Perhaps I was already sensing that there was a good deal of truth in Jeane Dixon's prophecy.

I had a strong sense that I wanted to establish something of lasting beauty. I wanted, somehow, to establish a bulwark against the worst kind of changes. I wanted to hold back ugliness and vulgarity somewhere if I could, and Wakaya gave me that possibility. As well, I suppose, I had a sense that I would need a place to which I could return to take stock and make plans. And to heal.

All of this proved to be true—truer than I could ever have imagined. Wakaya would come to mean much more to me than a tropical retreat.

It was a place greatly beloved by my only child, Erin. And my love of Wakaya is deepened by my memory of how much it meant to her. Erin loved the many places in Fiji we visited during our holidays together. She particularly loved the children of Wakaya and the other islands of Fiji.

I lost Erin one terrible night in December 1983. And so my obligation to conserve Wakaya and create a place of opportunity for its people is a way to honour her memory. More directly, Erin's unfulfilled dream of becoming a teacher has led me to focus my philanthropy on preschool education. This was a decision that Jill and I arrived at after my first unhappy effort to vent my grief.

After Erin's death, when Jill and I were still living in the Bahamas, I undertook to raise money for a school established in Erin's memory, for the children afflicted with blindness in the Bahamian Out Islands, but the experience was miserable.

(After marrying, Jill and I had not decided where to settle, so had stopped for a few years at Lyford Cay; we eventually sold that home to Sean Connery.) This was a situation that Erin had discovered and that had upset her enormously—children kept in appalling conditions, kept, in some instances, literally under the floorboards of their homes, treated little better than animals because the families viewed this tragic genetic condition as a direct curse of God.

On behalf of the Salvation Army, an organization that was already very effectively on the ground in the Bahamas, I sent out an appeal—one aimed primarily at our neighbours in the privileged compound of Lyford Cay. Jill watched me grow more and more bitter as members of the Lyford Cay community—people who were worth many millions of dollars and who lived only a short distance from the terrible suffering we wanted the school to address—contributed embarrassingly small amounts to the cause. There were a few instances of great generosity. Douglas Bassett, a Canadian businessman, and not even a resident of Lyford Cay, sent me a cheque for $25,000. But what I recall most vividly was the response of three of Lyford Cay's wealthiest residents—Sir John Templeton (who had recently got his knighthood by making a five-million-pound donation to Oxford), John Loeb Sr., the prominent Wall Street investor, and Henryk de Kwiatkowski, each of whom, by a coincidence wrote cheques for an identical amount.

In the case of de Kwiatkowski, I accompanied a Salvation Army major to de Kwiatkowski's Lyford Cay residence, and after showing us his Jacuzzi under a waterfall, boasting about Calumet Farm and the great successes of his race horses and polo ponies, and offering the (non-drinking) major a flute of Dom Perignon, he handed the major a folded cheque and bade us good night. The major was so excited by the financial resources that were so obviously at de Kwiatkowski's disposal, that he asked me to stop my car, under the lights of the Lyford Cay clubhouse. There he eagerly unfolded the cheque. There was silence, and then without a word he handed it to me. Like Sir John Templeton and John Loeb Sr., de Kwiatkowski had found it in his heart to part with $100. The major was so disappointed he could hardly speak. And Jill and I learned our lesson.

We would devote ourselves exclusively to the cause that we had chosen—in our case, preschool education. Jill and I wouldn't ask anyone for money. We would pay for the schools and for their maintenance ourselves. We would be creators, not fundraisers. As a result, we politely decline invitations to fund-raising balls and galas for other causes. Our energies and our money go toward building and running our preschools. We are single-minded and self-sufficient in support of the cause we have taken up in Erin's memory.

Erin had a strong instinct about the importance of education. Even as a young woman she seemed to have an implicit understanding of H.G. Wells' famous observation: "Human history becomes more and more a race between education and catastrophe."

There is a little poem of which Erin and I were both very fond. It goes something like this: "If I were a bird and lived on high, I would lean on the wind when the wind came by, and I'd say to the wind as it took me away, that's where I want to be today." I think of that poem—and of Erin—whenever we open a new preschool. Whether in Fiji, or, as a result of my association with the charter schools founded by my friend, the tennis star Andre Agassi, in Las Vegas, or in San Diego, Erin's memory is what helps me keep my focus. I have no personal connection with San Diego or Las Vegas, nor have any interest in funding the creation of vanity buildings. But long ago I learned to lean on the wind where the need is, and not where my ego is going to get a lift.

I'm certain that my partners at Southern Pacific thought I was mad when I proposed to them that I buy Wakaya. What was I going to do with an island in Fiji? I'm not sure that I could have given a very cogent answer back in the 1970s—and yet by then, I had watched enough, I had listened enough, I knew myself well enough, and I had enough of a sense of the gathering forces of the future, to trust my instincts. In the same way that I jotted down quotes because I guessed their wisdom would come in handy, I bought this island because I had a strong intuition that it would come to mean the world to me.

In the summer of 1942, I spent my holiday in northern Ontario, at a summer camp run by the gym master of the well-known Toronto private school, Upper Canada College. His name was Cochrane, and it was often called Cochrane's Camp. Officially, it was Camp Temagami, and it was situated in the land of lakes and great wooded forests that an Englishman named Archibald Belaney had already made famous in books such as *Pilgrims of*

the Wild and *Tales of an Empty Cabin*. Of course, Archie Belaney wasn't the name his many readers knew him by. In 1998, Richard Attenborough directed a film about his life, starring Pierce Brosnan, and it used, as its title, the name by which this strange, mysterious man was much more widely known: Grey Owl.

"The calm and silent presence of the trees," as Grey Owl described Temagami, was a truly majestic landscape. I remember the adventure of heading out from the camp on a canoe trip with our packs of supplies, bags of flour and sugar, and a reflector oven for the haute cuisine that could be managed by a group of boys in the wilderness.

The Temagami area is a vast maze of lakes and rivers. There were bears to worry about, moose to see, bass and pickerel to catch. There were blue, cloud-billowed days and storms that came out of nowhere. "Dear Mom and Dad," I wrote. "I hope you are as well as I am. This morning we played bace ball with 26 boyes I was one capton and we wone by 39 poants ... we do a lot of canewing up her at camp...."

I am still deeply touched by something I discovered after my parents' deaths: that they kept all my letters from camp. And even if the "canew" trips didn't do much for my spelling, they were a great method for teaching self-reliance.

The lesson we learned at camp was as simple as it is profound, and it is this: that if we didn't manage to start a campfire in the rain, or get our tents pitched in a storm, or paddle down a long arm of Lake Temagami with the wind and waves against us—nobody was going to do it for us. It's a lesson I've often wished my friends on the left would take to heart. I can't tell you how many times in my business life I've thought of what those canoe trips taught me. A difficult meeting, a crucial negotiation, an important decision, a calculated risk—in all these cases, there's always the truth of a canoe trip staring me in the face: Nobody is going to do it for me.

Dad came to Camp Temagami that summer for a visit. This was an enormous event for me. Being the youngest in the family, and being a good deal younger than my sisters, I had a relationship with my father that was a combination of love, enormous admiration, respect, and yet some distance. He was usually busy with his work, and he came from a time when a man did not involve himself as intimately in the lives of his children as a father does today. I suppose I was aware of the distance between us. But I'm sure I wasn't the first son to wish at times for a closer relationship with his father.

I respected him, and hoped always to win his approval. But his professional success, his prowess as a sportsman, his military heroism, and his comportment as a gentleman made him a daunting example to try to follow. I think of him as an extraordinarily impressive figure today. Imagine how overwhelming he must have appeared to his young son.

I like to think that the inspirations on which I've followed through in my own life—the idea to marry good, elegant design with electronic appliance; the realization that an environment as pristine as Fiji's could produce the best bottled water in the world; the conviction that Wakaya's virgin, organic soil, so rich in nutrients, would produce organic crops and livestock of remarkable taste and nutritional value; the belief that a child's earliest education will be the foundation of everything that follows, and my determination, as a result, to make preschool education the focus of my charitable giving; the determination to make Wakaya a place where its natural beauty will never be threatened; the realization that computer technology provides the key to the future of the publishing industry—are all an inheritance from my father.

He didn't leave me a fortune, but he left me something far more important. He left me with the knowledge that a solution to a problem doesn't have to be fraught with complexity. Often a solution is surprisingly simple. Often, it is right before our eyes. All that one has to have is the courage to see clearly and to act.

As you might well imagine, the arrival of this mythic figure at a summer camp was quite an event for a boy—an event that I'm afraid I built up enormously in my imagination. I was almost giddy with excitement as the day of Dad's visit approached.

I'd planned that we would go out on an overnight together. It would be so wonderful to spend time with him alone! We'd paddle together. We would make camp. We would build a fire, cook our dinner, and sleep in our tent. I pictured myself sitting up with Dad in front of our campfire and talking into the night. I'd played the scenario over and over in my mind.

But at the last minute, Dad ran into a friend who also had a son at the camp and who had a cottage nearby—the only cottage on the lake, as bad luck would have it. We were invited to spend the night there, and my father—totally oblivious to the import to me of the outing I had planned—accepted. Of course, it made much more sense to him to spend the night in a comfortable bed rather than in a tent. I don't think he ever knew how I felt, because, of course, I couldn't let on to him how terribly disappointed I was.

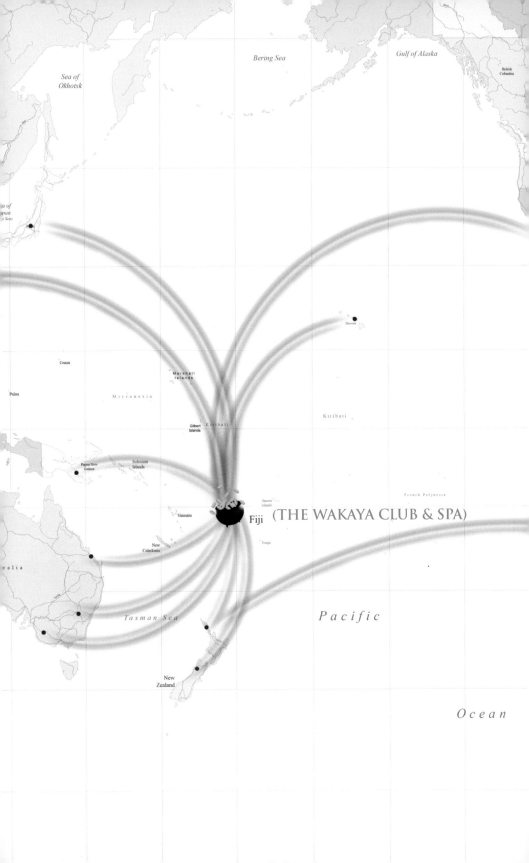

Fiji (THE WAKAYA CLUB & SPA)

THE ELEGANCE OF SIMPLICITY

"Success is not final. Failure is not fatal. It is the courage to continue that counts."
—Sir Winston Churchill

PETER MUNK AND I MET IN 1952.

We were young men, but it was clear to both of us, even then, that we were an unusual combination of shared enthusiasms and distinct personalities. In the kind of place Toronto was in those days—a little dull, a little narrow, and far from cosmopolitan—the differences between a Jewish émigré and someone from an established WASP family were often what created divisions between people. They had exactly the opposite effect for Peter and me.

I often think that it is the differences between us that made our partnership work so well. A partnership is not the same as a friendship—although, almost miraculously, Peter and I have enjoyed a friendship as well as a history of joint business ventures. A partnership of identical strengths and identical weaknesses is a partnership with an exceedingly good chance of ending in disaster.

Peter and I frequently disagreed, but disagreement was

a component of our working relationship. A disagreement was often the first step toward the successful refinement of an idea. Peter and I had a rule that is the very foundation of successful collaboration. When a business decision was being discussed, neither of us could leave the room until, after careful and complete debate, we had arrived at agreement. The animating idea of Clairtone was the result of just this kind of give and take.

Peter and I were both at the beginnings of our careers when we met. Peter, having graduated from the University of Toronto, was pondering the options that were open to an electrical engineer. He could see that breakthroughs in technology—from vacuum tube to solid-state; from clunky turntables to Garrard's sophisticated record-changer; from monaural sound to stereo—presaged a revolution in home entertainment.

Peter's prediction fitted perfectly with my own certainty that consumers were becoming too discerning and too sophisticated to be happy with the horrendous design that was so distinct a feature of electronic appliances in those days. The revolution of Scandinavian design had convinced me of that.

If I have a particular gift as a businessman it is that I am observant. It's a lesson my father taught me. Listen when you'd rather be talking, and watch when you'd prefer to be watched. It's advice I cannot commend too highly to any young person, and one of the results of my father's guidance is that I developed an ability to catch sight of trends just before they begin to become apparent to others. This isn't clairvoyance. It's not magic. It's really only the ability to pay attention, and to put pieces of observed information together in a new way. What this boils down to, in the marketplace, is the ability to see what people want before they know they want it.

Peter and I batted a few ideas back and forth, as we have so often in our lives. And out of our combined visions of the future, Clairtone was born.

Clairtone was a good idea. A very good idea. But lots of people have good ideas. The test of entrepreneurs is whether they act on good ideas. With the possible exception of some politicians I might mention, almost anyone can have a good idea. What an entrepreneur does is more than just dream things up. An entrepreneur is an alchemist who transforms an idea into reality.

Clairtone ceased to exist as a company in 1971, a few years after Peter and I left. That period was a sad, downward spiral, the unhappy end of a journey that began with dazzling success, and that made unmistakably clear why the public sector is, at best, an unreliable partner in enterprise. And even though the journey's conclusion was not at all what we had hoped—and even though there were some pundits who gleefully predicted that my partner Peter Munk and I would never get up off the ground after rising so high, so quickly, and falling so abruptly—it is a venture I now look back on with pride. The Clairtone team created something extraordinary. As well, the experience taught us many important lessons.

The story of Clairtone is the story of a partnership. It's a partnership that incorporates a close friendship, but it's important to distinguish between that and a friendship that includes a business relationship. I don't underplay my affection and respect for Peter Munk by saying that our relationship has always had the adventure of the entrepreneur as its essential medium—and not, say, golf, or sailing, or a mutual fondness for sports cars or football. We seem to communicate best in the realm of business ideas and business plans. That just happens to be our shared language, and we both take enormous pleasure in our discourses.

Looking back at the Clairtone days, I can see how many things we did right, and how many things we did wrong. We were very young, after all, but capitalism, like politics, makes no allowances for well-intentioned inexperience. Peter and I paid the price for heading into an enterprise with equal parts ambition and naïvety. Still, Clairtone is a persistent memory, and not just for me.

Almost 40 years after the company's demise, there is a permanent display of Clairtone products at the Design Exchange in Toronto. And to this day, the Clairtone team gets together for an annual luncheon to reminisce about what we achieved.

What I am most proud of is not the design awards Clairtone won, although that is something to be proud of indeed. To this day, Clairtone record players are collected by vintage hi-fi aficionados. People still remember Clairtone's unique look, and in a way that belies the decades that have passed since the Clairtone Sound Corporation's demise, the ideas that inspired Clairtone live on. Forty years later, Clairtone—a product that has been defunct for 40 years—has its own website (http://www.clairtone.ca/). In 2008, the Design Exchange in Toronto mounted an exhibition of

Clairtone products, and that same year a handsome book entitled *The Art of Clairtone: The Making of a Design Icon* was published. In the 2009 documentary film *Objectified*, the international design superstar Karim Rashid listed the Clairtone hi-fi unit he owned as a boy as a seminal influence on his thinking about how objects should look and function.

Nor is my pride primarily based on the fact that Peter Munk and I went from being virtual unknowns in the Canadian business community to being a pair of young entrepreneurs the press referred to as the Gold Dust Twins. In Clairtone's first annual report, our monthly sales figures were $23,000; in our second year $63,000; and in our third, more than $300,000. The numbers may not be exactly staggering, but their direction shows that we were obviously onto something. Our instincts about what the public was ready for—what, in fact, it was looking for—were proving to be right on the money.

We seemed instinctively to know the value of good marketing, and from the beginning we were aware that our ad campaign had to be as contemporary in feel and as unique as our product. This is a lesson that remains critically important, whatever the product. I sometimes wonder why this lesson is so often forgotten, only to be rediscovered again. It's not just what an ad says that's important, it's how an ad says what it's saying that matters. It's the "how" that must be truly reflective of the product in question; otherwise the message, however informative, will be lost.

As it happened, Marshall McLuhan was formulating his groundbreaking ideas about communication at the University of Toronto at the same time that Peter and I were working on the marketing scheme for Clairtone. There must have been some-thing in the air. I can't say that we were likely to be mistaken for philosophers, but McLuhan might well have made a fine ad man. "The medium is the message" is a brilliant encapsulation of the ad philosophy that Peter and I were feeling our way toward.

Our advertisements—inspired, to a considerable degree, by the work that I had done with David Ogilvy in New York during my Dansk Design days—were so original that people remem-ber them still. Dalton Camp, our brilliant Canadian advertising man, won an Ad Council Award for the Clairtone campaign. Clairtone was endorsed by the likes of Tony Bennett, Dizzy Gillespie, Carmen McCrae, and Oscar Peterson. To this day, people remember our most famous line: "Listen to Sinatra on Clairtone stereo. Sinatra does."

Our ads used the drama of empty space to wonderful effect. A full newspaper page with few words not only caught the modernist mood of the day, it also caught attention, which was the point. We needed the ad to grab customers, not to provide data. We needed the ad to be what I call a call to action—that is, a message to our potential customers that they needed to get themselves to the hi-fi section of their local department store to see this dazzling new product. Once they were there, the battle was half-won. The details could follow.

A new and startlingly unique product. A revolutionary ad campaign. A dazzling start-up. These were all impressive achievements. But what I look back on with the greatest pride is the simple fact that underlies all of Clairtone's successes. That Peter Munk and I, at age 29 and 25 respectively, acted on an idea.

We might have talked about it, and talked about it some more. And then, eventually, we might have got bored with talking, and we might have forgotten about it altogether. We would hardly have been the first young people to have let a bright and original idea slip away. But we didn't.

Why? What was it that made us special? We were, on the face of it, rather typical young men—interested in playing tennis, in skiing, and as obsessed with pretty girls as much as anything. Neither Peter nor I had exactly set the academic world on fire. And yet I think there was something remarkable that happened when the two of us came together. I think we were one of those combinations of qualities, talents, skills, and experiences that prove to be greater than the sum of their parts. To this day, Peter and I can set out on a walk through midtown Manhattan (as happened not long ago) and find that we have overshot our destination by ten blocks because we have been so engrossed in our conversation. In our early days, we had to stop taking vacations together because our young wives could scarcely get a word in edgewise once Peter and I were chasing down an idea. The simplest way I can describe it is that we spark off one another.

By the time I met Peter Munk, I had an eclectic CV. To say the least.

I'd worked as a boat boy at a summer resort in Ontario called Bigwin Inn. (It was there that I met Anna, my first wife.

She arrived for a dance on a Saturday night in the summer of 1949. It was one of those lustrous evenings that can be such jewels in the brevity of a northern summer. She was very beautiful as she stepped from the boat, and shockingly young, I realize now. She was 14 and I was a mature and worldly 18-year-old. She made quite an impression, and I suppose that the boat boy made more of an impression on her than her date did: We were married seven years later.)

In 1951, I volunteered to join the Governor General's Horse Guards, a Canadian regiment with roots reaching back to the Fenian Raids and the Riel Rebellion of the 19th century. It had served valiantly in both world wars, and it is the sister to the British regiment, the famous Royal Horse Guards. I realize now I was part of a continuum that saw nearly every male in my family serve in the military, from the Crimean War to the Boer War to the Natal Rebellion to the first World War. How quietly they all served and sacrificed. I believe America would be a far stronger society if we, like many other nations, required all our young men and women to serve their country.

As well, I had worked as a pot and pan salesman in Montreal, a job that, despite its unglamorous stature, taught me many useful lessons about salesmanship and marketing. Then, following my return to Toronto in 1952 from Montreal, I established myself as an importer of Scandinavian furnishings.

My company was called ScanTrade, and my first client was my sister, Shelagh. She had returned from Norway in the late 1940s. She had two children by her first marriage, and two by her second. Sadly, both marriages failed, but Shelagh was a remarkably strong and talented woman. Not only did she raise her family of four children on her own, she started her own business. She began with a small gift shop tucked in behind the Park Plaza Hotel in Toronto, and eventually expanded to what would prove to be an extremely successful store on Bloor Street called Shelagh's of Canada.

The youngest of my three sisters, Diana, had been obliged to take on the role of babysitter when I came along. She was the dearest companion for which a brother could ever wish. But when I was older, it was Shelagh, the eldest of the three, who took on the role of mentor, advisor, and confidant. In many ways, she was very much like my father. An excellent horsewoman and a real old-fashioned adventuress, she had her own unmistakable style. She also had a real knack for business. She had the kind of panache that allowed her to open a store that was pretty much a reflection of her own curiosity and spirit. Because of the time Shelagh had spent living in Norway, her store was the first in Canada, and one of the first in North America, to promote Scandinavian design. Shelagh was a businesswoman, Diana was an artist, and my middle sister, Pamela, was a poet. I am blessed to have learned so much from each of them.

I'd already been struck by the beauty of contemporary Scandinavian design. I recall, in Copenhagen, being bowled over by furniture, fabrics, and glassware—a revelation that was to have a direct impact on my career. It was the revelation of Scandinavian design that eventually led to Clairtone.

Sometime in the early 1950s, I found myself idling away a few moments in a living room in Toronto. Whose it was, and why I was there, are now long forgotten. I happened to be looking at what was supposed to be a good record player of the era. I'd been in dozens of similar living rooms, and had stood in front of dozens of similar record players. But for some reason, on that occasion, some questions began to take shape that I had not asked before.

The record player—high-end, for its day—had a high-gloss finish, and brass piping, and a plastic logo, and hideous gold lamé grill cloth covering not-very-good speakers. It looked like a cross between a casket and a brothel bar, and it screamed "appliance!" Why, I wondered, would anyone want an appliance in their living room? It was like having a fridge in the library.

In my imagination, I placed this apparition of bad taste beside some of the elegant Scandinavian furniture designs with which I'd become familiar. The comparison wasn't good. And this passing query—why did record players have to be so ugly?— proved not to be passing at all. It was the first glimmer of an idea. Fortunately, I didn't let it slip away. It wasn't so very long before Peter Munk and I began to ask the same question together.

On my trips to Norway, Denmark, Sweden, and Finland, the contemporary look of Scandinavian design had really caught my attention. This, in itself, was unusual. It wasn't as if I'd been particularly interested in design before. I doubt I could have told you the difference between Colonial and French Provincial. I can't remember ever being in a dining room in Toronto and saying to myself, "My, that's a nice salad bowl." Or, "What an interesting-looking set of wine glasses."

I suppose I had absorbed the basic tenets of good taste while growing up. My parents' mock Tudor house on Oriole Parkway in Toronto was beautifully, if conservatively, decorated. There were lots of lovely prints and English antiques—Chippendale furniture and an Adam sideboard. In the drawing room, a portrait of my father in his hunting pinks—a painting that now hangs in my study in Palm Beach—was hung across from the fireplace and two wingback chairs. The davenports and armchairs were deep and comfortable and upholstered with the kind of softly faded chintz that you might have seen in an English country home.

But, as is the case with most boys, I think, the elements of design that surrounded me were more or less invisible. They just were the way things were. I didn't really think about design much, to tell you the truth. And like most of my contemporaries in Toronto, and like the contemporaries of my parents, I felt that if you wanted to buy a wedding gift for someone you simply went to long-established gift and jewelry stores such as (in Canada) Birks, Ellis Ryrie, or Eaton's. Inevitably, you bought a cut-crystal vase, or a sterling silver ashtray, or a Victorian-looking cookie dish.

Things were different in Scandinavia. From kitchen utensils to domestic decoration, to furniture, to tableware, to appliances, to fabrics—a "look" was emerging that really caught my eye. I was there three years before the famous "Design in Scandinavia" touring exhibition took North America by storm. It wouldn't be until 1958 that an equally popular exhibition, "Formes Scandinavian," made the same big impression in Paris.

I was coming to all this completely cold, and yet I could see immediately that the uncomplicated and functional products being created by designers such as Stig Lindberg, Sven Palmqvist, Arne Jacobsen, Aro Vater, and Hans Wegner were the way of the future. Their work was vibrant, compelling, clever, and unconventional. It was also elegant, but in a way that was often arresting, amusing, even fun.

I was totally fascinated by the artful combination of traditional materials and the minimal forms that could be created with advanced technologies. Form-pressed wood. Plastics. Aluminium. These were not luxury items, even though they were stylish. In Copenhagen, in Helsinki, in Oslo, in Stockholm, you didn't have to be rich to have the most sought-after tableware, the most up-to-date furniture, the most au courant draperies and upholstery and bed linens. Frequently what was so revolutionary about Scandinavian design was that it was created by the technologies of mass production. This was a long way from the world of Waterford crystal, Limoges, and Wedgwood china from which I had come.

Big sister Shelagh loved mixing things up. A stone Buddha on a rustic Italian bench. Moroccan pillows on a French settee. Contemporary Danish tableware on an antique harvest table. This is not so unusual now, but it was then. Interior designers usually made it their business to impose a single "look" on the homes of their clients.

Shelagh took a different approach. She encouraged her clients to attune themselves to their own sense of beauty. She made it clear that eclecticism could be a good thing in an interior, a very good thing, so long as it expressed the lives and the tastes of those who lived there.

Her timing was very good. Shelagh's of Canada was a great success, in part because she had correctly guessed that Torontonians were ready for a style of decorating that was more worldly and idiosyncratic than had seemed possible to them before. Toronto is now a very sophisticated city in terms of design and home décor, but I don't think it is an exaggeration to say that a history of the emergence of this cultural confidence would include more than a passing reference to Shelagh's of Canada.

Shelagh's style was quite revolutionary in its day. It was successful, in part, because it stood out in such marked contrast to the uniformity of approach that was the hallmark of so much interior design at the time. Interior designers were often rigid in the looks they imposed, and were often successful at convincing clients that any idiosyncrasies were best bulldozed by the expertise they had hired. You had a Victorian home? Then everything had to be Victorian. You favoured English Country style? Then everything had to be chintz and Persian carpets. A Georgian settee in that modern bungalow? I'm afraid not.

Shelagh would have none of it. For her there were no obligations of a look or a style so long as it was beautiful. Her confidence was infectious, and it taught me about more than interior design. It reinforced an element of my business philosophy that was already beginning to take shape: An entrepreneur can learn from experts, but he need not rely on them. Shelagh's example helped me learn the value of believing in my own instincts. This is among the most important lessons, of life and of business, that I have ever learned. It is a rule of thumb that has always stood me in good stead.

Shelagh insisted on an aesthetic order that was much more self-defined, and it is interesting to me that her approach, so unusual in its day, has become the norm of elegant interior design. Flip through any architecture or design magazine, and it becomes clear that, for enhancing a lifestyle and stimulating the imagination, the eclectic exuberance to which Shelagh was naturally drawn rules the day.

Scandinavian design remained central to Shelagh's store, and ScanTrade took on the role of importing the products she needed. Every year I headed off on buying trips to Denmark, keeping an eye open for furniture, glassware, pottery, stainless steel, and fabrics. It's hard to imagine, now that downtown Toronto property is as valuable as it is, but ScanTrade had a barn-like warehouse directly behind Shelagh's Bloor Street store. And that was the centre of my operations. ScanTrade had a staff of two, one of whom was me. But gradually, as Scandinavian design proved to be ever more popular, we expanded our client list from Shelagh's of Canada to national stores from coast to coast. Eaton's, Simpsons, Ogilvy, Birks, and the Hudson Bay stores carried our products.

The names of those stores will be lost on most non-Canadian readers. It's not surprising. Canadian institutions are, as they say, world-famous in Canada. But frankly, I think there are worse places for a young entrepreneur to begin. Canada is a particularly instructive nut for a young business person to try to crack.

It's not exactly easy making a go of it in Canada. The land mass is larger than that of the U.S. and the population is smaller than California's—a combination of characteristics that means that national sales do not always add up as profitably as they might in more densely populated countries. In fact, I recall an article in *Fortune* magazine that pointed out that the CEOs of 20 major American corporations had one curious biographical detail in common: They were all from Winnipeg, my place of birth. The point of the article being that Canada is a rigorous training ground for executives. If you can make it there, you can make it anywhere.

By 1954, ScanTrade's national sales were going well. I was relieved to see that the banks seemed content. As well as operating ScanTrade, I became one of the associates of Dansk Design. There were two partners—American and European— and although I didn't have the money to be an investor, I was an active associate, and I covered Canada.

Dansk Design was really a marriage of some exciting trends in design that were coming out of Scandinavia and some of the older, long-established European manufacturers who were looking for ways to reinvent themselves after the war. For example, solid teak was becoming extremely popular, but it was also very expensive. Dansk Design saw a way to employ the elegance of Scandinavian design with some old-fashioned techniques.

We found a company that made butter barrels and pork

barrels, and we realized that we could use the same staving technique to create beautiful bowls, trays, ice buckets, and carving boards. They looked very elegant. They had all the warmth and richness of teak, but because they were not solid, they could be sold at a very attractive price point.

In the same way, we found a company that made dappled blue and white tin enamelware of the sort that you might see in a cowboy movie or around a campfire on a canoe trip. We came up with some new designs and some bold colours, and we helped our manufacturers adapt to this new line of production. In keeping with the casual elegance of Scandinavian design, we created a casserole pot with a lid that could be turned upside down and used as a trivet, so that cookware could be brought right to the table as a serving dish. This became very popular, and before long we were producing one of the most successful giftware lines in North America.

I was learning some lessons (usually by trial and error) that have stood me in good stead ever since. For one thing, I learned that establishing a brand quickly was of paramount importance. Creating a coherent design group, or failing that, creating the illusion of a coherent design group, was a huge boon in marketing. I insisted that our products be displayed together, rather than spread in various departments throughout a store, some in kitchenware, some in gifts, some in flatware and tabletop. This strategy created a demand, not simply for an item, but for the look the brand defined. And once the brand was established, I did whatever I could to burnish its reputation. For one thing, I avoided discount retailers whenever possible. I tried never to deal with outlets that would lower the prestige of the product. Part of what we were selling was mystique, the notion that owning our products enhanced one's own prestige. This is difficult to do if that same product is being sold at rock-bottom prices at factory outlets and retail clearance operations.

Something else I learned was the importance of product exposure—in magazines, and in films. This was then, and remains today, an extremely effective form of communication. Something we did very well, years later, with FIJI Water. Whatever it cost to get bottles of our water to a table where Brad Pitt would be sitting—and, as a matter of fact, the cost was never really that great—the investment was worth every penny.

Creating visibility is critical. Everything follows from that, and for Scandinavian designers, there was no more effective way to do so than to have Michael Caine, in *The Ipcress File*, make his coffee in a Danish plunger, a device few North Americans had seen. Product exposure works hand in glove with a good advertising campaign—which was the other lesson I learned. Just as a product is reflected in the movie stars and celebrities who are seen using it, the quality of a product is expressed by the quality of the ads. But then, I had a very good teacher.

It was during my time with Dansk Design that I encountered the advertising genius David Ogilvy. We met in New York. He was by then becoming one of the most famous names on Madison Avenue, and David's influence on marketing and advertising is still significant. We knew he was good, of course. But I sometimes wonder if we realized how enormous his impact would be. As an undisputed master of marketing, he had an enormous influence on me.

I was altogether in awe of him, to be frank. An obvious contrarian, he had a tremendous presence and a keen intellect. Scholar-like, and with an amazingly imaginative mind, he was quite eccentric in some ways. But his copywriting was legendary. His line, "At 60 miles an hour, the loudest sound in this new Rolls-Royce comes from the electric clock," is still considered by many a masterpiece of marketing.

Like me, David Ogilvy never finished college. He followed his instincts, and they led him along an unconventional route. He worked in the kitchen of a hotel in Paris, where he learned "discipline and management." Then, like me, he became a door-to-door salesman, although his product, the Aga Cooker, became rather more of an institution than mine, Century Metalcraft. He seemed to be a restless spirit. He tried polling, and then farming, before he moved to New York to set the advertising world on its head. But once he committed to advertising, his talent was such that the business was never the same again. General Foods, Lever Brothers, and American Express were a few of his bigger clients. And Dansk Design was one of the smaller, if not the smallest.

It was his insistence on the power of simplicity in advertising that influenced the ads that we later ran for Clairtone. A striking photograph, bold type, a clever headline, and a minimum of copy. To this day, people still remember opening the customarily-staid pages of the Toronto *Globe and Mail* and being bowled over with the striking effect of a full-page ad that had far more white space than text.

This approach was almost unheard of at the time. The prevailing wisdom was that if you were paying for ad space, then you'd better fill the space with words. David Ogilvy understood—as did Dalton Camp, the Canadian ad man who later headed up our Clairtone campaign—that providing information wasn't the purpose of an ad. An ad is about inviting people in.

What an ad had to do, first and foremost, was catch people's attention. This—the creation of visibility—I came to realize, was the first of the three steps of what would become my marketing mantra. The second step is trial. People have to try the product. The third is advocacy. Once they try it, they spread the word about how good the product is. But the first—and the step from which the other two follow—is visibility – continued visability that ensures a product is not out of sight and therefore not out of mind! Nothing works in the world of marketing unless people know that a product is there. And making things visible by making things striking, or amusing, or dramatic was what David Ogilvy was all about. To establish the brand: Therein lies the first step in creating wealth.

In fact, this was a lesson I had learned, in the most curious way, some years before. It was during my time as a young pot-and-pan salesman in Montreal. In those days, I was often in the company of a young and devilishly handsome sculptor named Jim Ritchie. Jim and I were soul mates in many ways: illustrative, I think, of the fact that an artist and an entrepreneur are not as far apart as many people might imagine them to be.

We were both dreamers and both schemers. We both had a kind of confidence in ourselves that was not always easy to explain. We were both obliged to marry the impracticality of living entirely on our imagination with the extreme practicality of figuring out how to do so. Both of us were intent on pursuing a career path that many people assumed did not exist. And both of us managed, against considerable odds, to stick to our guns. I still remember to this day Jim remarking, "An intellectual is a man who says a simple thing in difficult way, but an artist says a difficult thing in a simple way."

Despite some considerable family pressure, Jim was resolute in his refusal to go into the family business. It was a soft-drink company. Jim politely but firmly resisted his family's overtures. He headed off to Europe at his first opportunity. Like so many artists, writers, filmmakers, actors, and, yes, businessmen, Jim had realized that Canada was simply not big enough to support his ambitions.

And he was right. He is now a well-known and successful sculptor. He has lived and worked in Vence, in the south of France, for more than 50 years. In 1994, my wife Jill and I were staying at the Chateau Saint-Martin hotel in Vence, and, on the spur of the moment, I looked Jim up in the phone book and gave him a call. We hadn't seen one another in decades, but it was as if no time had passed at all. We had lunch. We visited his studio. And now one of his most beautiful pieces stands in pride of place in our garden in Palm Beach.

But it was Jim's father who taught me an important lesson in marketing. Mr. Ritchie knew a thing or two about maintaining a commercial presence, and one of his most artful schemes was at a time when the family business was doing very poorly; when, in fact, Ritchie Ginger Ale was very close to bankruptcy. When less imaginative businessmen might have been trying to save gas money, or hoping to knock a salary off the payroll, Mr. Ritchie instructed a driver of a Ritchie Ginger Ale delivery truck—an empty delivery truck—to drive back and forth on the highway between Montreal and the resort area of the Laurentian Mountains. This was an inexpensive way of advertising, but more importantly, it gave people travelling on the Laurentian highway a sense that Ritchie Ginger Ale was a bustling, busy going-concern.

I've often thought of that empty delivery truck. With Dansk Design, with Clairtone, with FIJI Water, and certainly now with Wakaya Perfection, when a national advertising campaign was either unaffordable or (as was the case with FIJI Water) not strategically advisable, I realized that giving local customers and retailers the impression of a national campaign was, in many respects, just as good as having one. When an ad for Dansk Design appeared on an easel on a floor in Bloomingdale's—an enlarged reprint of the ad that had appeared in *The New Yorker*—it never hurt that it gave the appearance of a nationally advertised product. When our ads for Clairtone appeared in the Toronto *Globe and Mail*, they were big and striking, and as a result many people assumed that the same ads were appearing in newspapers across the country. This never hurt.

We took a page from Mr. Ritchie's playbook with FIJI Water when, in New York, we turned a minivan—one minivan—into a replica of FIJI Water's trademark bottle, and had it drive up and down Fifth Avenue and Madison Avenue.

Friends would say to me, "I saw one of your fleet of vans today."

From a marketing point of view, the aura of success is often more useful than success itself. Like Jim Ritchie's father, I've never underestimated the value of perception.

From the day we met at a popular Toronto restaurant called Diana Sweets, I think Peter Munk and I knew we were going to somehow join forces. To be honest, Peter's first attention to me, his future friend and partner, had more to do with my very pretty date than with me. But eventually, it seems, I came into focus for Peter, and then, as now, we sparked off one another.

It wasn't perfectly clear to us, but in hindsight it's easy to see that we both brought very different skills to the table. "David can smell a product or visualize an idea," Bill Birchall, the man who became our partner in 1969 in Southern Pacific Hotel Corporation, once said. "And Peter can make it commercially viable." The fact is, during the first years of our friendship—during the period of parties at a big old house we rented on Roxborough Avenue, and ski weekends in Collingwood, and bowls of spaghetti bolognese at a Toronto restaurant we favoured called Old Angelo's—we were both immersed in the two different streams that would eventually combine to become Clairtone.

Putting his engineering degree to good use, Peter had established Peter Munk and Associates. With a staff of two employees (one secretary and one technician) he was busy installing custom-designed high-end audio visual units in Toronto homes, and although it obviously wasn't going to make him a millionaire, his business was thriving. Part of the service he provided was essentially disguising the existence of the not-very-attractive hi-fi components in living spaces—in cupboards, in antique cabinets, in walls and ceilings. Essentially, his customers wanted to have music—good, clear music—in their residences without tripping over wires or stumbling over speakers. Peter made this happen.

But more importantly, the trend that Peter had discerned, and on which he was capitalizing, was something more than electrical interior design. What Peter had sensed were the first dim glimmerings of what we would now call the home entertainment industry. He had a hunch that there was, or soon would be, a growing market for reasonably advanced sound systems in homes. This was prescient. If you stop to think that the 1950s were not all that far removed from the days of the family Victrola and a stack of 78s, and if you consider the surround-sound home theatres, CD and DVD players, plasma screens, satellite radio, and the wired, high-tech living rooms of today, it's clear that Peter was on the ground floor of what would prove to be an enormously lucrative business. This is typical of Peter. His instincts are always shrewd.

Peter Munk had discerned that the shifting demographics of the post-war era, the relative affluence of North American life, the increased sophistication of consumers, and the advances in technology (many of which were fringe benefits of the war) were all pointing toward a new and extremely profitable market. "Modern living is the rediscovery of the pleasures of living at home," Peter wrote in one of his early flyers. "Many of us have found adequate dwellings, a little spare money, and some leisure time at our disposal." In that uncomplicated statement there was a wealth of economic and sociological observation. He was onto something—something big.

I have a vivid memory of my sisters, my mother, my father and I, sitting in the living room, listening to the one household radio, on December 7, 1941. And I remember to my astonishment Dad leaping to his feet and cheering. I didn't understand why such bad news would be greeted with such enthusiasm. But my father knew at once. He realized what the bombing of Pearl Harbor meant. He meant no disrespect. He was an ex-soldier himself, and no one would have been more aware of the grief felt by American parents or wives or children for whom the Japanese surprise attack on the U.S. Pacific Fleet was the day they lost a son, or a husband, or a father. But he realized at once what the results of Japan's offensive would be. Britain was already fighting, of course, as were Commonwealth countries such as Canada. The war, for us, had started in 1939.

In our living room in Oriole Parkway we listened on our wooden-cabineted radio to Roosevelt's grave speech. It was indeed "a date which will live in infamy," but it was something else as well. There was, in FDR's voice, a tone of grim determination. It was clear to my father that a slumbering giant had been awakened. The Americans were in. Until that moment I think he had feared that England would be lost.

We gathered around that radio to listen to *The Lone Ranger,* or *Amos 'n' Andy,* or to hear Winston Churchill's stirring speeches during the war. The radio. That one, central radio. And now here I am, like everyone else, with my iPod, and satellite radio, and wireless speakers, and DVDs and CD players, and flat-screen televisions. That's an astonishing transformation, in less than a lifetime. Perhaps only the computer revolution would mark a more impressive upward curve of product growth than the home entertainment industry.

To anyone not privy to the conversations that Peter Munk and I were beginning to have in the early days of our collaboration, it must have appeared that our businesses were in different worlds entirely. Different universes, even. It must have also appeared that the same wide distinction was true of us. I was the son of a well-known and established Toronto family, comfortably off and blessed with the confidence that comes with such a background. I didn't have a trust fund on which to rely, but I had a certain social comfort level with people who had money or access to money. They didn't make me nervous, or anxious, which meant, a little later on, that when we were looking for investors for Clairtone or for Southern Pacific Hotels, I could speak from what appeared to be a position of strength. We were never going cap-in-hand; we were always offering investors an extraordinary opportunity. And my being at ease in boardrooms, in beautifully appointed corner offices, in exclusive clubs, or in the drawing rooms of the best addresses was a quality that Peter realized could be put to good use. In our early days, my background helped me feel, when I entered an impressively appointed room to meet with potential investors in Toronto, in New York, in London, or in Hong Kong, that I belonged there.

Peter, on the other hand, had no such safety net. He was very much on his own, and was blessed with the energy and drive that comes from knowing that his success would depend entirely on his own efforts. I didn't always acknowledge my safety net, I suppose, or pay much attention to it. I may even have rebelled against it in my way. But the fact that it was there was a defining element of my personality. Just as the absence of a safety net defined Peter's. We really were yin and yang.

And here, I think, is the first point of my unlikely conjunction with Peter Munk. As different as we were, we were both attuned to what was new and to what was exciting. We were both looking not at what was right in front of us, but at what was on the horizon. Timing is everything in business, and whether we were aware of it or not, we were both testing the wind for new trends and direction. And from a business point of view, we were looking ahead for a perfectly straightforward reason. The future was the turf that nobody else had yet claimed.

I often say that all I do is look for what's missing. Both Peter and I were beginning to realize that what we needed to do was to introduce products to the market that was just on the very brink of realizing it wanted. It's a tricky balancing act; you want to be ahead of the wave, but not too far ahead. The Studebaker remains the classic example of a good product that was just a bit too far ahead of its time. And to find the sweet spot between invention and consumption, you have to rely on what no school can teach. You have to pay close attention to your instincts.

It's interesting to think how unlikely a confluence of talents and interests Peter Munk and I must have seemed when we met in 1952. What common business interest could an electrical engineer and an importer of giftware find? It's even more interesting to think how obvious and natural that coming together seems now, in hindsight. And that's what's at the core of entrepreneurialism. It's the transformation of the unimagined into the inevitable. Clairtone was a great adventure. It was almost as if it was an enterprise that was waiting for the two pieces of the puzzle to come together.

Perhaps the spirit and excitement of my first partnership with Peter Munk was best summarized in an article written by the financial editor of the *Toronto Telegram* in the autumn of 1958.

"It was just over 11 months ago," wrote Devon Smith, "that their outfit, Clairtone Sound Corporation Ltd., tried its wings. The product was a hi-fidelity, stereophonic piece of equipment for the home. It combined the electronic engineering of Peter and the furniture designing of David. These boys … don't admit to any business genius. As a matter of fact, president Peter Munk shows a marked awe of the business know-how of his sales manager. But after quizzing them you begin to realize that if these men have a motto it is: why not? For instance, why not make a beautifully finished stereophonic set for under $500 that has more features than those at double the price? They've asked a lot of why-nots in the past year-and-a-month. And they keep getting outrageously successful answers."

Why not? It's a good question.

When Steve Wozniak and Steve Jobs began building computers in Jobs' parents' garage in California, I doubt anyone thought they were going to change the world. Anyone, that is, but them. Change the world? They must have glimpsed the extraordinary possibilities that were opening up in that plain, everyday garage, and asked: Why not?

As career beginnings go, it was not very auspicious. Or, at least, it did not appear so.

Long before I met Peter Munk, when I was just starting out, many of my peers were on their way to lifelong careers with brokerages, or law firms, or banks. Over drinks at the Toronto Club or in the dining room of the Badminton & Racquet, proud fathers were telling one another about sons starting out, and doing famously, thank you, at Wood Gundy, or Osler Hoskins, or the Canadian Imperial Bank of Commerce. I, on the other hand, had taken a route that did not give my father much in the way of bragging rights with his friends over their scotch and sodas. I started out by selling pots and pans.

"Pots and pans, you say," was probably the best my father's friends managed. "How interesting." And the slightly vacant expressions, the awkward silence, and the gently rattled ice cubes that accompanied this comment must have eloquently expressed the conventional wisdom concerning my prospects.

The job was in Montreal. For a company called Century Metalcraft, out of California. They were, in fact, quite good pots and pans. Hammered-aluminum castings with Pyrex glass lids that were able to cook food quickly and thoroughly without boiling everything to death. A good, solid product. They were sold, not in retail outlets, but by door-to-door salesmen—of which I was the youngest.

My market was primarily working-class Montrealers, people who had little money to spare, and who would likely only spend it if convinced that an investment was a good one. And it was my job to knock on their front doors and talk my way into their homes so that I could do the convincing.

At the time, I'm not sure I would have been able to articulate exactly why I had decided to head off to Montreal to sell for Century Metalcraft. It's hard to know how young people make the career decisions they do. How can anyone know in advance of any real experience that they're going to be a good doctor, or a good lawyer, or a good business person? Or even know what they want seven years hence. And yet somehow young people sense the way for themselves. Based partly on hunch, partly on instinct, and partly on hope, a chosen direction is often a leap of faith as much as anything. But now, with the long view of more than five decades of hindsight, I have to say I think my instincts were correct. In Montreal, I got a very useful degree, one in grassroots marketing.

Somehow I knew that selling and marketing would both play a prominent role in my future, and so it seemed to make sense to take on a job that required me to do both. And my job with Century Metalcraft proved to be a crash course in the fundamentals of commerce. The most essential elements of both sales and marketing are present in the brief (sometimes very brief) exchange between a door-to-door man and a potential customer. I'm not sure that there is any kind of sell that is more difficult than the cold call, and standing on a small front porch in a work-ing-class neighbourhood can be about as cold as a call can get.

I must say, it didn't hurt that those doors were in Montreal. I am someone who feeds off the energy of the places where I've lived. In 1948, and then in 1952, I had spent many months trav-elling in Europe before returning to Canada, and I had fallen in love with London, Paris, Rome, Barcelona, and Madrid. Often dreary, often joyless, Toronto did not compare well.

Montreal was different. Montreal was a little bit of Europe in North America. In Montreal, in 1952, there were sidewalk cafés, espresso bars, restaurants, and late-night jazz clubs. There was La Tour Eiffel with Johnny LeBlanc at the piano. There was the Maritime Bar at the Ritz Hotel. Wine was part of the fabric of Montreal life, whereas in Toronto buying any wine or spirits in the ghastly provincial liquor stores had all the pizzazz of getting a prescription filled at a hospital dispensary.

But my Montreal adventure did not begin in a blaze of commercial glory. It became quickly apparent that I required a marketing scheme beyond the minimal instructions I had been given. Ringing a doorbell and starting to talk when a suspicious face reluctantly appeared did not work quite as wonderfully as one might have hoped. And here was the first of the business lessons taught by my experience selling pots and pans: There's nothing like a few slammed doors to get you to rethink your marketing strategy.

The goal was simple: a sale. And the route to the goal turned out to be extremely direct. I was beginning to formulate what would become my marketing credo: Visibility creates trial, which creates advocacy. If you make a potential client aware of a product, and then you put the product convincingly through a trial or a demonstration, not only will you create a customer, you will create a customer whose very ownership of your product will advocate on your product's behalf. Of course, this assumes that what you are selling is worth selling.

To be perfectly frank, I'm not sure what I would do if ever I were called upon to sell something in which I didn't believe. The world does not need more hamburgers or ball caps or bobble-head figurines and that being the case, I'm not the man you want to have selling them. There are people who are exceptionally gifted at selling anything. It's not the product, it's moving the product that drives them. They can sell, whether or not they believe in what they are selling. It's salability, not quality, that is important for them.

For me, the opposite is true—and in the future, the opposition of quality vs. disposability will be even more stark and critical for the entrepreneur to discern. Whether it's a high-end stereo system, such as Clairtone, or a superior source of water, such as that found amid the volcanic highlands and tropical forests of the Yaqara Valley in Fiji, my starting point has always been my belief in a good product. You might smile (as I'm sure my father's friends smiled), but pots and pans were no exception.

The vital questions for a door-to-door salesman on the sidewalks of Montreal to address were: If I managed to get beyond an abruptly slammed door, how did I get their interest, and once I had their interest, how could I create a demonstration? It's not as if I could cook them their dinner.

And here, let me provide a brief insight into the mind of an entrepreneur. Could a hi-fi unit be both well made and beautifully designed? The answer: Why not? Could FIJI Water someday become an internationally-recognized brand and a real competitor with giants such as Evian and Perrier? The answer: Why not? Could subscriptions to digital magazines replace the dusty piles of *New Yorker*s and *Economist*s and *Newsweek*s that are piling up in households across the country? Why not?

"It's not as if I could cook them their dinner." Why not?

Cooking dinner for my potential customers was my simple and, as things transpired, totally effective marketing plan. A housewife would hear her doorbell ring at eleven o'clock in the morning. She would answer the door of her modest Montreal home, there to find a neatly dressed, perfectly polite, entirely presentable young man who would say hello and apologize for interrupting her day. A polite, presentable young man who would then make the most surprising offer.

The young man informs Madame that he'll cook dinner— cook dinner for her and for her husband. He will buy the groceries, prepare the dinner, serve it, clear, and clean up. The kitchen, so he promises, with an appreciative glance around the neatly-kept home, will be left totally spotless. And the young man, who the housewife is finding to be most respectful and pleasant, wonders if perhaps there are some friends who might like to join them. Another couple or two, perhaps? Neighbours? Relatives? He'd be more than happy to accommodate. Any evening they might choose.

And so, night after night, in working class neighbourhoods in Montreal, I arrived at homes with two suitcases of Century Metalcraft pots and pans and the groceries required for a dinner—usually for six. Chuck roast. Vegetables. Potatoes. For dessert I featured banana pancakes and maple syrup. My grocery budget was always five dollars; I made certain that I showed them the bills at the end of the evening. And they were always suitably amazed.

Almost invariably, the people who welcomed me into their homes were courteous and charming. Many of them were Polish immigrants, and before very long the evening felt, even for me, more like a dinner party than a sales pitch. Developing empathy with potential customers is key, and I've always had a knack for it. Still, I kept my eye on the ball. No matter how much I was enjoying the company, I had work to do. Many times since, I've watched sales or business people, intent on selling a product, or finding an investor, or clinching a deal, build a pitch beautifully, and then walk right past the moment when the hammer should have dropped. Whether this is some kind of shyness, or lack of confidence, or a reluctance to get directly to the nub of a transaction, I've never really understood. But I've always tried to keep that moment very much in mind as it approaches, so that when it presents itself, I'm ready to act.

I demonstrated how to prepare the vegetables with only a little water and salt, so that they were not overcooked. And how to roast an inexpensive cut of meat so that it was tender. After the meal, I cleaned up thoroughly, as promised. The manner I assumed was that of an amusing butler. And then, while my new friends were in a relaxed after-dinner mood, I slipped into sales mode. I got out my flip charts and explained how Century Metalcraft pots worked and how they were made and why, even though a set of nine was certainly a bit of an investment—$230, as I recall—they were not only going to help create some truly delicious and nutritional meals, they were, over the long term, going to help the household save money. They were also, I explained, going to help people live healthier lives. Vegetables would no longer be boiled to death.

It worked. I received a letter from H.P. Dwyer, Vice-President, Century Metalcraft Corporation in Los Angeles, that I still have in my possession. "Your activity in the month of February is deserving of great praise. You have done a wonderful job … and are to be sincerely congratulated." Why not?

I can't recall when Peter and I asked the fateful question. Nor does Peter. But it must have been over one of those bowls of spaghetti at Old Angelo's, a Toronto restaurant we liked in large part because in those days it was one we could afford. Or perhaps it was in front of the beer fridge in the rented house on Roxborough Avenue that had become a kind of clubhouse for our group of friends. Or on a ski slope in Collingwood. Or on a tennis court. Wherever it was (somewhere unmarked by a historical plaque, I am quite certain), I asked Peter the fateful question. Couldn't hi-fi units be beautiful? Why not?

Otherwise they had to be hidden, or they had to be owned by people who were indifferent to appalling wood veneer, garish logos, fake escutcheons, and the tacky gold screening that so often covered speakers in those days.

At the time, I was asking this question about a lot of household items as a result of my exposure to Scandinavian design. Why did kettles have to be so ugly? Why did everyday tableware have to be so dull? Why did contemporary furniture have to look so second-rate?

The stainless steel flatware of Scandinavian design, the teak furniture, the glassware, the linens—all taught me that good design did not necessarily have to mean expensive.

It was only natural, I suppose, that I should eventually ask Peter about ugly hi-fi units. And it was only natural that Peter (always the big-picture guy) should pick up on where my questioning was headed: It was headed toward our future.

"Everything I've been able to achieve afterwards is because of Clairtone," Peter has said. "The biggest thing I got from the whole experience is self-confidence. I can achieve anything I set my mind to. We learned that the impossible is attainable."

We were busy with other aspects of our careers, to say nothing of being busy with the various excitements a young man's life can provide. I was married and living in the Toronto suburb of Thornhill. (Eventually, after the deaths of my parents, I purchased the inherited family home from my sisters and moved into Oriole Parkway.) Things were humming along very satisfactorily with ScanTrade and Dansk Design, although I had to admit that even then I knew that becoming the biggest importer of giftware in Canada was not a goal to which I wholeheartedly aspired.

Peter and I were becoming increasingly convinced that we were onto something, and sometime in the spring of 1957, we committed to the idea. We worked with our electronic technician, Michael Chojnacki, to make three preliminary models of what would become the Clairtone line. We imported the first cabinets from Denmark and had them assembled at a small factory in North Toronto.

Then in September 1958, we rented a suite for an evening in the Park Plaza Hotel in downtown Toronto in order to show our new product to buyers from leading retail outlets. The hotel had recently completed a wing to the north of the older hotel. (The Park Plaza was a Toronto landmark. And I'm amused that longtime Torontonians still refer to the section built more than half a century ago as "the new part.") It was a much more contemporary design than the older section, and we made sure that our suite was there. Being new, we realized, was what we were all about. Somehow, instinctively, we understood that everything should send that signal. Here is the description by

Garth Hopkins, author of *Clairtone: The Rise and Fall of a Business Empire*, of the sets we had on display that night: "Compact chassis with high-quality components and good speakers housed in a low-slung Scandinavian-style cabinet with sliding doors. Oiled walnut finish. No flashy chrome or metal bits to detract from the clean, pleasing lines." Something like that couldn't be shown off in any old hotel suite.

We didn't need publicists. We didn't need a team of salesmen or a bevy of pretty girls to meet and greet the people to whom we wanted to show off our creation. We only needed Peter Munk, me, and the Clairtone models. And, frankly, based on our success, I couldn't see any reason to adjust this philosophy. Of the buyers who gathered in the hotel room that evening for our demonstration, all 11 placed orders.

Eighteen months later, Clairtone was a national business success story. Our marketing campaign was the talk of the advertising world. The Beatles, and Frank Sinatra, and the Prime Minister of Canada all had Clairtones. Peter Munk and I were being interviewed by every newspaper and magazine in the country. Clairtone was the subject of a colour spread in *Canadian House and Garden*. Peter and I both had more invitations to give speeches than we could manage. And I often wondered if those friends of my father who had been so pessimistic about my prospects ever connected the dots. I wondered if they ever figured out that I was the one who launched my career in Montreal, selling pots and pans door-to-door.

As is sometimes the case, it takes a real bang on the head to drive home the basic fundamentals of life—and of business. And if ever you feel you need to learn a lesson in such a vivid way, let me tell you, the several-hundred-pound hatch of a Sherman tank really does the trick.

In 1951, the year before I met Peter Munk, I joined the Governor General's Horse Guards. It is the sister regiment of the Royal Horse Guards. Its regimental march is "Men of Harlech." Its trot is "Keel Row." Its motto is "Nulli Secundus"—"Second to None"—and the braided epaulets, short jacket, true pants, and spurs of its dress uniform were splendid. It suited me perfectly.

It remains one of the strongest reserve regiments in Canada. Today it has troops in Afghanistan and in other trouble spots throughout the world. I am enormously proud of my affiliation, and 60 years later, my time in the Horse Guards stays with me.

It's hardly fashionable advice these days. Young business people expect to be in university one day and on Wall Street the next. But I'm not sure there is better training for business, or for life, than military service. Once you've experienced a forced 48-hour march, or have stood up to your knees in ditch-water, you know that a little discomfort is not cause for complaint. Once a drill sergeant has said to you, as one said to me, "Should you pass out on parade, you will, without fail, not drop your rifle. You will protect your rifle by falling under it. Is that understood, Gilmour?"—you will be perfectly clear about consequences and about responsibilities. I don't think many young people today, excluding those who have served, ever receive orders quite so unequivocal.

Once you've kept going even though you are wet and cold

and tired, you see things from quite a different perspective. After my service, I knew that, however great the discomfort or hard the work, I'd survived worse. It's a good thing to know.

I sometimes wonder what would have become of me had I not trusted my instincts and joined the army when I did. Discipline, of course, was the great lesson—and discipline, at its essence, is doing what you need to do, when it needs to be done. In the army there are orders to be followed, whereas in the civilian world, orders are replaced with goals, with ambitions, with the demands that are required of us if we are going to fulfill our own aspirations. But in the end, it doesn't matter whether the motivation is an officer's command or a self-appointed responsibility—it's the response that is important. There is no such thing as "not right now" in the army, and interestingly enough there is very little room for it in business. The Horse Guards came along at precisely the right time in my life. My time in the army provided me with tools I've used throughout my professional life. I doubt I shall ever repay my debt.

In the fall of 1951, we were out on manoeuvres. I was commanding a troop of four tanks, and I was standing in the open hatch when we went over a more sizeable bump than all the other sizeable bumps we'd been going over all day. Whether it was a maintenance error, whether I had not secured the hatch carefully enough when I took my position, or whether some piece of the equipment broke, I'm not sure. Whatever the cause, the hatch came down with a wallop that knocked me out cold as it pounded me to the steel floor below. My crew hoisted me up, and carried me out to the side of the track we were following. I wasn't in the best mood when I came to.

An expression of gratitude toward that hatch was not one of the many colourful expressions that crossed my mind that day, but I have to say that I've always thought it provided me with a useful tip. I had left things to chance—to the chance that someone had done their job, or to the chance that I had pushed the hatch back correctly. I didn't check all possible exigencies, and I paid the price. There's a saying that goes: "If you lose, don't lose the lesson." As a businessman, I often have reminded myself about that tank hatch.

Clairtone was in many ways an exercise in trying to leave nothing to chance. At first, nothing escaped our attention. The tiniest design details. The subtlest change to an ad. We worked with the sales staff of retail stores to make sure they understood our product, were comfortable demonstrating it, and knew how to clearly explain its unique attractions. We even helped set up their displays.

We made sure our service department was efficient and dependable. And we established an operational philosophy that I have tried to maintain since. We invested in our people, not in prestigious office space in high-rent locations. Our headquarters were modest, to say the least. Everything we did right was about maintaining control.

And what we did wrong was about losing it. Because Clairtone's runaway success was so dramatic, and because we were young and inexperienced, it was difficult at times to keep things together. We were eager to create the kind of success that would make the world sit up and take notice. For example, in

1959 our sales into the American market were pretty much equal to those of the entire Canadian radio industry into the American market in the previous year. Even then, Peter and I sensed that the future was more global than domestic. This truth was particularly clear when the domestic economy in question was Canadian. One aspect of Canadian policy that drove us to distraction in our Clairtone days was the wall of import duties, a policy that only served to protect the mediocre domestic copies of foreign invention and designs.

But our domestic sales were expanding almost exponentially. Clairtone was the subject of articles in magazines and newspapers, as were its two happy, if exhausted, young owners. We'd expanded our facilities and our staff. It was a great success story.

But as all business people know, sudden success is a very mixed blessing. If you have x sales in June and (because of the buzz that has surrounded June's sales) you have enough orders for $4x$ sales in October, how do the June earnings pay for the greatly expanded production, transportation, and personnel costs that the pending October triumph will require? What about inventory? What about unpaid accounts receivable? Throw travel and marketing expenses into that puzzle, along with the cost of building new facilities, designing new models, and sustaining a larger payroll, and you can see that Clairtone was not immediately the bonanza that people assumed it to be. In fact, it was rather like having a tiger by the tail.

The company's prospects looked brilliant, but prospects don't always butter the parsnips. We were borrowing money so that we could keep growing. I had moved into the family home following my mother's death in 1958, and in order to keep throwing fuel into Clairtone's chugging locomotive, I took out a mortgage on Oriole Parkway, practically for its total value. Peter often reminds me, with some amazement, that I did so without asking him to co-sign or take any responsibility for the loan. But it never crossed my mind. We were both so focused on our goal that we never bothered with tallying up the values of our respective commitments. We were giving it our all—which is what entrepreneurialism demands—and I simply happened to have an asset that could be used to our advantage.

People cautioned us against expanding too quickly. But neither Peter nor I were very interested in slowing down. As Peter told the writer Donald Rumball, "I work better under pressure. If I had cash flow problems I would never have slowed down. No way! Our job was to solve the problem, not take the easy way out."

Less than 18 months after we sold our first unit, we went into partnership with Irving Gould, one of the first Canadian venture capitalists, and Clairtone went public. At first issue, Clairtone's share price was $2.50. By March 1961, shares had risen to $12. Things were looking very good. Peter and I could now afford to eat somewhere other than Old Angelo's, not that there were many places in Toronto at that time that were very much better.

How ambitious were we? Well, just as I had no real interest in becoming the biggest giftware importer in Canada, Peter and I had no interest in becoming the most successful record player producer in Canada. At least that was not our ultimate goal. That was always going to be a step along the way. But the

American market beckoned. So did the British. "Entering 1962," so that year's annual report stated, "the company was facing the most dynamic period of its short history with expansion in every facet of its operations. Economical production was essential to face growing competition from all quarters if the company was to seize a dominant position in world markets."

But as exciting and as promising as all this seemed to be, it's possible now to look at it from a different perspective. It was all pretty heady stuff, especially for two young men. At the height of its success, Clairtone was the hi-fi to have. Hugh Hefner had a Clairtone! In some ways, and on a much smaller scale of production, Clairtone might be compared to the iPod of today: an excellent, brilliantly designed product that, through the alchemy of creative marketing, becomes a "must-have."

But the same story could be told from another point of view. It could be seen as a steady loss of our control. And loss of control means an increasing inability to leave nothing to chance. We didn't know it, but the hatch of our tank was about to come crashing down on us with a mighty wallop.

Finally, after eight years as the Gold Dust Twins, Peter and I were obliged to walk unceremoniously away from what we had created. We were both shattered to have worked so hard at something only to watch it evaporate. And the lesson that neither of us would ever lose was this: We had made the mistake of aligning ourselves with interests that diverged from ours—in this instance, the provincial government of Nova Scotia.

Curiously enough, it was my oldest and best friend in

Canada, Peter Hunter, a comrade-in-arms from my days with the Horse Guards, and a former Full (as well as Honorary) Colonel of the Regiment, who unwittingly helped to facilitate our deal with the devil. In his capacity as a board member of Toronto's Empire Club, he was hosting Robert Stanfield, the Premier of Nova Scotia, while he was in Toronto to give a luncheon speech. Stanfield's government had been in discussion with Peter and me for some time about bringing Clairtone operations to their province, and Stanfield wanted to close the deal. He asked Peter Hunter if he could make use of a room in the Royal York Hotel for a meeting he needed to have, and Peter, of course, complied, never guessing that the meeting would be between Robert Stanfield, Peter Munk, and Peter's old army chum, one David Gilmour.

The government of Nova Scotia had seen us as the kind of innovative corporation it wanted to attract. It was desperate to modernize and diversify its economy, based as it was on the traditional resources of fish, forests, and mines. We, at the same time, were desperately in need of stability and sustained cash flow, and because the financing being offered appeared so attractive, we accepted. But what had seemed so hopeful in that room at the Royal York proved to be far from the triumph we had imagined. "Don't give away your destiny," was the lesson Peter and I learned. Because suddenly we were no longer in control. Suddenly more than a few things were left to chance.

Of course, we were young and resilient. But we were also focused—focused on success. One of Dad's favourite sayings was that it's not the strength of the wind, but the set of your sails that determines the way you go. A young entrepreneur could do worse than to take to heart my father's old saying. Peter and I understood it implicitly.

Peter's genius was in preparation. The searching out of contacts and potential investors and the presentation of a proposal was my department. We made a very good team. Over the years I've often heard Peter say that it's not necessarily genius that explains success. It's focus. And the two of us certainly had that in spades.

But by 1968 those triumphant days were behind Messrs. Munk and Gilmour. The details of the story may be of interest to business historians, but the cogent point is this: We aligned ourselves, and left ourselves open to, forces that did not share our ambitions or goals. The government of Nova Scotia was more intent on improving employment figures than on manufacturing an excellent product. The unions, obviously, shared none of our objectives. These forces pulled in a variety of directions, and as a result the wheels came off. Clairtone foundered.

The press was not kind. We had overreached. We'd had our heads turned by our own success. We'd been greedy. It seemed that any time a reporter felt like getting some easy mileage, a column would appear that compared us to Icarus, the boy who flew too close to the sun. The stories were hard to stomach. But even so, it was helpful to remember what Churchill once said: "The press often consists of vulgarity divested of the truth."

Our truth was not something we would be able to read about in newspapers. The truth lay ahead. We had faith that it was there. We just weren't quite sure what it was.

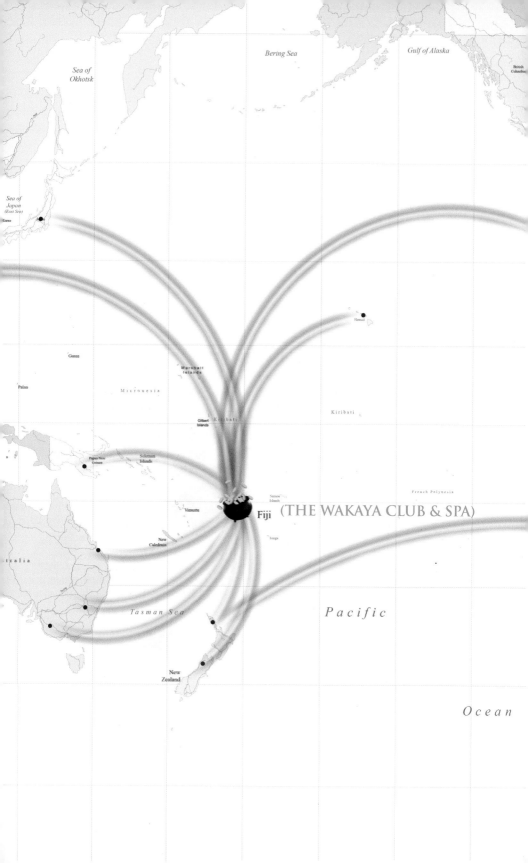

Fiji (THE WAKAYA CLUB & SPA)

REACHING FOR THE OUT-OF-REACH

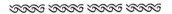

"No crime is so great as daring to excel."
—Sir Winston Churchill

So what went wrong with Clairtone?

When did the business goals to which Peter Munk and I aspired turn from what we reached for, to what we could manage, to what we could cope with—to what we hoped would let us get out with our shirts still on our backs? Did we—as Garth Hopkins suggests in his excellent book, *Clairtone: The Rise and Fall of a Business Empire*—expand too quickly into the American market? Timing being everything, were we too far in front of the curve on colour television? Should we have stayed based in Toronto, as our resident advertising guru, Dalton Camp, believed? It's difficult to say. Perhaps our problems were all of the above.

After Clairtone's demise, there were whisperings that dogged us for years. Rumours of mismanagement and bankruptcies and the sale of our own stock. Finally, impatient with these phantom accusations, we hired the renowned Canadian barrister Robert Macaulay to undertake a complete review of our

Clairtone years. When Macaulay accepted our brief, he made it clear that he would only do so if his inquiry could be entirely impartial, however well or poorly we might be portrayed in it. We accepted his terms.

His report was thorough, filed on February 22, 1974. "In short," it concludes, "as a result of our review of this matter, it is our opinion that any allegation of improper or wrongful conduct arising out of dealings in the shares of Clairtone Sound Corporation Limited on behalf of Mr. Peter Munk and Mr. David H. Gilmour are without foundation in fact or law."

Still, it remains a sad tale—at least, in its conclusion. The death knell for Clairtone came when we became associated with two forces—government and labour unions—that had very different agendas from ours. And here, I return to the idea of simplicity. In any company, big or small, everything and everyone must pull toward the same clearly identified goal. In this way, a good company shares the essential quality of good design. Form must follow function.

In later years, when, the goal was to become a well-known national brand within five years of launching a new product. Everything was geared to that. With Zinio, the goal was to become one of the digital world's most popular apps. The goal defined everything we set in motion to attain it.

Success is as simple as that. Have a well-defined objective—one that is shared by every member of the company.

Failure is what happens when objectives and agendas

become muddied, confused, and contradictory. It's a business rule that should never be broken: Only run with those who share your direction. But it is a rule that Peter and I broke at Clairtone. It was a lesson we took with us to our next joint venture, Southern Pacific Properties.

The truth is, I don't much care for most resorts. They seldom live up to expectations. They are usually too big, too obligated to the demands of mass tourism, and too diluted with economic compromise. My guess is that most people who holiday at large resorts don't get relaxed, they get rattled. Rattled because nothing looks quite as it did in the brochure, rattled because they have to open their wallets every time they turn around, and rattled because the staff often communicates, by way of a forced cheerfulness, that they'd just as soon throttle guests as serve them.

By the end of a stay—or perhaps, on the most miserable occasions, by the beginning of one—people end up wondering what was wrong with their own bed, or bath, or kitchen. The television in the next room is on all night, the housekeepers vacuum the hallways at eight in the morning, the scuba instructor does not inspire confidence, and the scrambled eggs are cold at breakfast. Wouldn't it have been better to stay at home?

It's unfair, I suppose, to blame resorts for being less than perfect. Perfection seems a little much to expect of anything. Particularly tourism. But that's just the problem. As unfair as it is, a holiday is always perfect in anticipation. Oh, it will be perfect, we dream. Then, of course, reality sets in. And my word for the reality of most tourism is … anticipointment.

Most people base their idea of perfection on childhood memories. The perfect day at the beach. The perfect birthday cake. The perfect toboggan hill. That's certainly true in my case. I can think of a perfect holiday I once had when I was a boy. I wonder sometimes how much that memory—a memory of something that simply couldn't have been better than it was—inspires me. I wonder how much it pushes me to reach for what is always just out of reach.

It was a summer during the Second World War when I was sent to stay with my aunt and uncle who owned a ranch in Alberta, in western Canada. I spent my days riding, almost always by myself. Sometimes I rode from dawn to dusk. I loved these outings so much that there were nights when I slept in the stable so that I could saddle up and get an early start. For a young lad who lived in the city but who dreamed on a much more wide-open canvas, it was indeed perfection. Certainly, it was perfect freedom.

The life of an entrepreneur is fraught with risk and uncertainty, but the upside is freedom. You might have to pay a price for this freedom, and there may be days when the pressures are such that you wish that you had a regular job with a regular pay cheque. (The last six months of Clairtone spring unhappily to mind; so does the memory of Peter and I watching a project called the Pyramid Oasis disappear into the Egyptian quicksand during our Southern Pacific days.) But in the end, freedom is what lies at the heart of a life in which every day is a new adventure. Rebels and artists, wanderers and inventors, creators and entrepreneurs all drink from the same well.

I developed my taste for freedom during that perfect summer out west when I was a boy. Setting out in the brisk, fresh mountain air with a whole day stretching before me and with no one to tell me where to go. Mt. Eisenhower, Three Jewel Lakes—this was the world that was mine to explore. In those days, the Canadian Pacific Railway maintained cabins on the back trails. They were a day's ride apart, and all you were required to do to use them was leave them as clean and tidy as you found them. I was free as a bird. It was a holiday right out of a *Boy's Own Annual*.

Shadow was my horse that summer—my aunt had given me the responsibility of grooming him, feeding him, and mucking out his stall. This was a job I undertook with great dedication. She insisted that I care for Shadow as if I actually owned him. That's exactly what I did, and at the end of my holiday, in return for fulfilling the responsibility she had given me, my aunt did the most wonderful thing: She presented me with a bill of sale. Shadow was truly mine. I was the official owner of a prized asset, and even though it was an asset that I would never see again, the pride of ownership is something that has never left me. It was also a good lesson in the obligations of ownership. There are duties to be fulfilled before there are dividends to be enjoyed. But the dividends are considerable.

As Shadow galloped across the brush range and over those twisting gullies, the wide, blue Alberta sky was before us, the white-crested mountains behind. I had only my dreams to keep me company.

Sometimes it was The Charge of the Light Brigade that Shadow and I re-enacted. Sometimes it was Custer's Last Stand. Sometimes I imagined myself with my father, a decorated war hero who, having been wounded several times and having survived the trenches of the First World War, returned to London, volunteered for the Dunsterforce and, in the months after armistice, embarked from Baku to fight with the White Russians against the Bolsheviks.

I often think how different this kind of childhood experience is from the computer screens and tweets, the video games and chat rooms that play so prominent a role in a child's life today. Of course, I see the enormous potential of the digital revolution—this awareness is what sits at the heart of my enthusiasm for Zinio—but I worry that when children are not encouraged to play, to roam, to dream on their own in the natural world, when they are not permitted to be by themselves and to invent their own narratives within the context of unstructured time, they will not develop the capacity for imagining that is the source of creativity. In his book, *Last Child in the Woods: Saving Our Children from Nature Deficit Disorder*, Richard Louv writes, "At the very moment that the bond is breaking between the young and the natural world, a growing body of research links our mental, physical, and spiritual health directly to our association with nature." The thinking of the entrepreneur is not so different from that of the artist, and both have their origin in the imagination of a child—in the kind of unsupervised, unstructured time that I was fortunate enough to experience on the mountain trails of Alberta during that magical summer.

Sometimes, as I rode Shadow and as the sky and plains opened before me, I recited the poem by A.A. Milne that I knew by heart, and that, many years later, I taught Erin, my daughter. It's a kind of mantra that I've recited to myself over the years, and it's been helpful in good times and bad. It's always reminded me that whether I was travelling alone in an unfamiliar place, or whether I was starting a business in an unfamiliar culture, there was no reason to be fearful. If you let yourself be taken by your own sense of adventure, rather than be intimidated by the unknown, there is nothing to fear.

I'd give Shadow a flick of the reins and a prod in his flanks, and off we would fly. And as we made our way toward the horizon, I'd repeat Milne's line to myself: "If I were a bird and lived on high, I would lean on the wind when the wind came by, and I'd say to the wind as it took me away, that's where I want to be today."

There are exceptions that prove the prevailing rule of resorts. Rare exceptions. I might go so far as to say, extremely rare. These are exceptions that, for the most part, are passed on by word of mouth—from the discerning to the discerning. They are almost like secrets, a kind of membership in a club. The club of those who, like Winston Churchill, are "easily satisfied with the very best."

The people who know these secrets, who are curious enough to seek them out and discerning enough to recognize them, are the kinds of guests we welcome at The Wakaya Club and Spa. Almost all are fascinating, although some are more well known than others. Celine Dion, Zubin Mehta, J.K. Rowling, and Tom Cruise have all been guests at Wakaya. Steve Jobs of Apple, Steve Case, the co-founder of AOL, and Bill Gates of Microsoft have all visited. Nicole Kidman came with Keith Urban. Mick Jagger has tried twice to come, but in both cases he wanted to stay at Vale-O, the secluded hilltop residence, and in both instances it was unavailable. But Keith Richards and Ronnie Wood came with their wives, and had a most pleasant holiday—until the occasion, during a beach picnic, when Keith fell out of a tree and had to be flown to New Zealand for treatment of a subdural hematoma. (A discreet sign on Honeymoon Beach marks the spot. It reads "Beware of Falling Stones.")

I've made great friends there. Don Vinson, a great American legal mind, is someone I met at Wakaya. Some of the most fascinating conversations I have ever been a part of have been around a table at The Wakaya Club and Spa.

Jill's and my home is contiguous with the resort property, although it is only a short walk away, and there is a seamlessness of natural beauty on Wakaya that makes guests feel part of a single lush and majestic landscape. As Jill explained to *Palm Beach Illustrated* magazine, "our goal is to create an extension of our own home, so that we could share this paradise with a few other people who could truly appreciate it." I describe it as the last bastion of sanity in a world gone mad.

I like to shock people with the audacity of what we are trying to do. "The idea is to try to create something perfect," I say when people ask me about our ambitions on Wakaya.

It's not an idle boast. It's not a slogan. It's not some glib remark we toss off without thinking very much about the implications of what we are saying. Jill and I know that perfection is impossible, but that doesn't mean it can't be our goal. That doesn't mean that reaching for it shouldn't be what we do. That's the simple reason why my newest start-up is called Wakaya Perfection—we are striving to grow and produce the very finest, most perfect wellness products on earth … an aspiration that is perfectly aligned with my prognostication about the coming consumer revolt against the disposable in favor of the permanent!

It is my belief that this urge, the aspiration to perfection, is part of the DNA of a successful entrepreneur. It has to do with both dreaming and hoping, but what it mostly has to do with is knowing how to work—hard—to make those dreams and hopes reality. Perfection, of course, can apply to many things: the perfect business proposal, the perfect deal, the perfect management structure, the perfect marketing scheme, the perfect product. A conductor must imagine the perfect concert. An actor, the perfect performance. I'm sure Andre Agassi still dreams of playing the perfect game of tennis.

All unattainable. All out of reach. Perfection is so frequently and so consistently proven to be beyond our grasp, it's no wonder that only romantics pursue it. And most creative capitalists, in my opinion, are romantics. Somewhere at the heart of all my entrepreneurial adventures has been the dream of attaining some kind of perfection. When I think of the revision-after-revision-after-revision that Peter Munk, our associate Bill Birchall, and I laboured over when we were preparing our proposals to potential investors for Southern Pacific Hotels and Resorts in the early 1970s, I realize that what we were trying to do, what we were obsessing over, was to make them perfect. I doubt that we ever succeeded. But not only does obsessing over getting things absolutely right make sure that … well, that things are absolutely right. It does something else that is very important for entrepreneurs trying to convince investors, or lenders, or potential partners to support a plan. It conveys passion.

Whether the start-up is record players, or hotels, or gold mines, or bottled water, or digital magazine distribution, or the purest, most healthful wellness products on earth like our Wakaya Perfection ginger and dilo cream, somewhere in our calculations and plans there is always the distant, beckoning possibility of bringing all the elements together flawlessly.

Such an ambition is overt at Wakaya. We make no bones about it, frankly—and the projects that we are working toward are part of this same quest. And while the resplendent beauty of an island in Fiji may seem a long way from the nuts and bolts of creating a product and selling it, I'd argue that entrepreneurs who don't have the idea of perfection sitting somewhere in their psyche are at a disadvantage. Business is not about the attainment of perfection, but it is about making sure that your entrepreneurial journey heads in the direction in which perfection lies.

☥

Southern Pacific Hotels and Resorts was seen by many of Peter's and my critics as a way of our getting as far away as possible from the demise of our first joint venture. But it was our sense of the future, not our disappointment in the past, that led us forward. Entrepreneurs are often contrarians, creators who don't so much swim against the tide as find their own new current. And Peter and I could see (contrary to the counsel of worried friends, worried bankers, and worried "experts") that the future was more global than domestic.

This truth was particularly clear when the domestic economy in question was Canadian. The Canadian market is small and suffers from over-regulated insecurity as a result. One aspect of Canadian policy that drove us to distraction in our Clairtone days was the wall of import duties. Peter and I both knew we needed to stretch our wings beyond the confines of Canada.

It began with a chance encounter with a mutual friend of ours who was the CEO of Volvo Canada, and who had been a pilot in the New Zealand Air Force during the Second World War. While chatting at a cocktail party, either Peter or I asked him about his ideas of business opportunities around the world.

"The Pacific Basin," was his immediate answer. Then he elaborated. "There's this place, a little dot, islands in the middle of the South Pacific. Wonderful people, wonderful place …

totally unknown. I fly down there on my way home to New Zealand frequently."

Peter and I were intrigued. All the more intrigued when he made a suggestion.

"Why don't you invest a little bit of money in a piece of real estate? There's no real estate tax, so it has no carrying cost."

And that was our toe-hold in the South Pacific. Eventually, I began to travel there to see the possibilities for myself. And that was the beginning of Southern Pacific Hotel Corporation.

But Southern Pacific was no wild guess. We didn't just roll the dice. It was a hunch—but not one of the shot-in-the-dark variety. Peter and I were good at talking our way through an idea—identifying it, refining it, addressing the obstacles that might stand in its way, plotting the course that would best bring it to fruition. And as our Clairtone dream was ending, we could discern—dimly, I suppose, and not without some risk, I admit—that the wheels of change were turning once again. We began to think beyond home entertainment. And we began to imagine that newly affordable air travel and leisure time might make an investment in hotels and resorts a smart move. We felt that this would prove to be true even in a part of the world that North Americans and Europeans thought of as impractically distant and extravagantly exotic.

Peter and I were also beginning to think a lot about an emerging phenomenon that would have an enormous impact on our business strategy. The word "inflation" had just begun to enter into general parlance, and we had an idea that it might be possible to have an investment that produced sufficient cash-flow to service debt but that would, at the same time, appreciate in value. We bet that a sea-change in travel, in leisure, and in real-estate investment was around the corner. It proved to be a good bet.

The Southern Pacific years were exciting, dramatic, and full of adventure and travel. It was Southern Pacific Hotels and Developments that introduced me to Wakaya Island, and that alone is enough to make me look back on SP fondly. Oddly, though, for all the exotic locales and busy itineraries, the business lesson that I most value from that period is the most down-to-earth of all. It was one taught not in Hong Kong restaurants or New York dinner parties, but over our desks and boardroom tables and during our long, coffee-fuelled, smoke-filled, late-night meetings.

At Southern Pacific, Peter and I, along with our partner Bill Birchall, made sure that we were always entirely prepared. Fanatically prepared, you might say. Our proposals, budgets, and business plans were revised and re-revised more often than I now care to think, so intent were we on making sure that they were always as good as they could be. Couldn't this sentence be clearer? Couldn't this illustration be stronger? Can't we improve on this headline? Wouldn't it be better if this diagram were on page two rather than page three? The three of us were never willing to sign off until we were certain everything was as nearly perfect as possible.

I was our man-on-the-road in those days, and whatever uncertainties may have prevailed in meetings with potential investors in London and Hong Kong, or bankers in New York and Sydney, I could always count on my presentation being rock solid. Charm can go a long way, but not nearly long enough in the real world. It can wear very thin, very quickly, if it isn't backed up with substance. At Southern Pacific we devoted an enormous amount of time to making sure our presentations were as impeccably prepared, as carefully thought through, and as beautifully put together as possible. And we made it a rule of thumb never to present an idea, make a pitch, or propose a budget until we were ready to make our presentation properly and convincingly. Timing is everything. It's an English term my American friends sometimes find a little strange, but we made it our business not to run off half-cocked.

Jill and I operated with the same obsessive attention to detail in the planning of The Wakaya Club and Spa. We made sure we had the vision clearly in our imaginations before we began even to think about construction. We wanted to be sure we got things right.

Jill and I mean exactly what we say when we are asked about our objective for Wakaya. Reaching for perfection: It's almost a motto. Still, I'm not sure our guests believe us—until they arrive. Until they have had their picnics on beautiful, entirely deserted beaches, mornings on the tennis court or golf course, afternoons spent snorkeling on the coral reefs directly in front of their absolutely idyllic seaside cottage-suites, spa treatments administered by gentle, quietly-spoken attendants while listening to gently breaking waves. They may have their doubts, until they experience the exquisite meals, interesting wines, comfortable, beautifully appointed accommodations, attentive, caring staff, and evenings spent watching the sun set over the distant islands of Viti Levu and Ovalau while sipping their flutes of Taittinger champagne.

There is internet access in our Wakaya Club villas and *bures*. But one of the most common comments from our guests? How lovely it is not to have a television in their rooms and accommodation. They tell me how good it is to hear themselves think. How productive it can be when things just quiet down.

It's not by accident that so many of our guests have had some kind of breakthrough at Wakaya. Whether wrestling with a business challenge, or a creative roadblock, or a personal problem, there is something about Wakaya—its peacefulness, its calm, its beauty—that soothes away the irrelevant. Wakaya puts things in perspective. More than that, it has an attendant clarity that puts ideas in view that were not in view before.

Wakaya is all about how truly exquisite simple pleasures can be. A sunset. A barefoot stroll on a deserted beach. A thought. The place operates in general with the same philosophy our staff employs in our kitchens. A meal is made with ingredients that are so fresh and good its preparation needn't be overly fussy or overly elaborate. Everything we are doing with Wakaya's agricultural programs is geared toward simply providing the best, freshest, most nutritional, and tastiest resources to our kitchen staff. But simple is not easy to achieve—the most ordinary flower is staggering in its beauty—but simplicity seems to be what makes me most happy. It seems to be the quality of life that I find most satisfying.

Our interest in good food, for example, and the delight we take in it, has helped make a visit to The Wakaya Club and Spa truly one of the best dining experiences in the world. Soon we will be self-sufficient in supplying our kitchen's needs, but with no impact on the island's peace and tranquility. No guest at The Wakaya Club and Spa will be aware of the few hundred working acres hidden in the interior valleys of the 2,200-acre island (2,000 of which have been certified as organic!) —unless, of course, they want to see what we are doing there. We raise our own Fiji Fantastic lamb, Peking duck, and many other crops. Neither turkey nor venison are imported. (Nowhere else in the South Pacific can an island boast of a 1,500-head herd of wild venison!) Our Wakaya Perfection organic ginger is, without question, one of the most remarkable products in the world and makes every dish just that much better! Our chickens supply our eggs, and we tend groves of what I consider to be the world's most succulent papaya. The combination of virgin, nutrient-rich soil and gentle, generous climate means that the fruit is not only delicious, the trees grow at an almost Jack-and-the-Beanstalk rate. All our fruits, vegetables, herbs, and spices—a garden that includes six varieties of lettuce!—are organically grown and nurtured in a pristine environment. No pollution is carried in the winds that reach us, there are no residues of chemicals in our grounds. An agricultural inspector told our team on Wakaya that he had never before encountered soil that was so pure, so virgin, and so rich in nutrients that he would gladly eat it. And it's absolutely true. Quite apart from the ecological and healthful benefits, you can taste the difference in the dining room.

Mentoring is important to us, and our guest-chef program has brought some of the great culinary geniuses of the world to Wakaya to enjoy a holiday, but also to pass on their expertise and recipes to our staff. Chefs such as the late internationally renowned Charlie Trotter of Chicago, Grant MacPherson of the Bellagio in Las Vegas, Masa Takayama from the Time Warner Building on Columbus Circle, and of course the extraordinary Nobu Matsuhisa. Their visits have been inspiration for the four gifted chefs who work in the kitchen of The Wakaya Club and Spa. (Four chefs to 14 couples being, you have to admit, a striking ratio.)

Jill's focus and attention to the details at Wakaya amazes me. I learn from it constantly. Of course, interior design rises or falls on precisely this talent, or lack thereof. But attention to detail is an extraordinary asset in the business world as well, one that I have tried to practice throughout my career. And I know a few executives, and more than a few politicians, who could improve their performance by simply studying my wife's uncompromising attention to Wakaya.

Her secret is straightforward. She simply treats every space she creates as a space in which she might live. In fact, she does live in them. She has stayed in every one of the free-standing suites at The Wakaya Club in order to make sure that everything, from the shower to the power outlets to the linens to the hangers to the bathroom amenities to the lighting, is exactly as she would wish it, were it her residence. She sees no reason why there should be any difference between an owner's standards and a guest's—which must be one of the reasons the two of us are so simpatico. I do the same in business. I try to make what I'm selling precisely what I would buy.

Peter Munk and I have both said, and only partly in jest, that we never became involved in a business that we knew anything about. When, in the wake of Clairtone, we set out to establish what became Southern Pacific Hotels and Developments, we knew very little about the South Pacific, and less about the running of hotels. But we could glimpse promise, and I am inclined to think that the excitement of great promise more than outweighs the anxiety of uncertainty. Certainly, that was always true of Peter and of me. From the time I first met him, Peter was a dreamer. But he was—and is—someone who dreams with a goal in mind.

Peter Munk had a presence that was immediately apparent on the afternoon in 1952 when I first met him. He was charming and charismatic. Qualities that, I would come soon to learn, he employed in both business and in his other principal preoccupation of the day: the seduction of extremely attractive women. He was not exactly tall, dark, and handsome, but what Peter lacked in leading-man looks—and what he lacked in capital and in experience as a businessman—he made up for with enthusiasm and a laser-like intensity of focus. This characteristic has not diminished with time.

Peter wasn't from Forest Hill or Rosedale. He hadn't gone

to Upper Canada College or Trinity College School. He hadn't played tennis at the Badminton and Racquet Club or signed for meals on his father's chit at the National Club. Things hadn't gone easily for him, and there was no path being smoothed by family and friends for his advancement. He was, perhaps, the first person I'd ever met whose future depended on nothing other than his own wits, and energy, and ambition. He attended the University of Toronto and graduated in 1952, at the age of 25, with a degree in electrical engineering.

Peter has often said, rather modestly, that he is not a genius, but he does admit to having a genius for focusing. The intensity he brings to bear on a project—or, in those days, to the women he was so avidly and constantly pursuing—is what has always separated him from the pack.

Those alert round eyes seemed to take in everything. There was something magnetic in his restless energy. There would be times when his intensity was mistaken for impatience, and part of my role in our early partnership was to reassure investors that Peter's drive did not contradict his levelheaded-ness. But his enthusiasm was amazingly seductive.

I came from a world in which people did not necessarily hunger for success, in large part because they were already so accustomed to its trappings. Peter was different. Peter Munk was always hungry.

Peter had been born in Budapest, and he spent the early years of his childhood there. The events of the war had seemed far away in North America, where we sat in our living rooms and listened to the news from Europe on our radios. Peter had not been so fortunate.

Although Peter's Hungarian family had been well-to-do, the war was devastating for them. They were Jews, obliged to flee Hungary in 1944—a dangerous and costly forced emigration. They left everything behind. Their train was bombed by the Allies, who had mistaken it for a military transport. Somehow, they survived this desperate adventure. And somehow, with little more than what they could carry, they arrived in Switzerland.

By the time Peter left Zurich to study in Canada in 1948, the Munk family fortune was, for him, a hazy memory of his grandfather's stately home in Budapest. His family no longer had much in the way of resources; they helped him as best they could.

There is a legend that Peter spent the $350 his family gave him for his university education on a beautiful woman he met onboard the ship that took him to Canada—and having observed Peter in action over the years, I'm quite prepared to believe that the story is true. Inside that crisp, business-like exterior there lurks the heart of a true romantic.

Peter had assumed that an uncle in Toronto would lend him the money he now needed for his tuition. As things turned out, this assumption proved to be more wishful thinking than fiscal reality. The uncle was not quite as willing as Peter had imagined to replace what had been spent so cavalierly on dinners and champagne. The uncle felt some reckoning was in order.

Peter had to earn his tuition money back by picking

tobacco near the town of Delhi in southwestern Ontario during his first long, hot summer in Canada. A tough lesson, but one he learned well. I don't believe he has made many inaccurate financial projections since.

I often think we have the best of both worlds at Wakaya—a private home, secluded and surrounded by nothing other than the physical beauties of sea, and sky, and breathtaking landscape. Or, we can be sociable, if we wish. The Wakaya Club and Spa is a place to meet some of the most fascinating and dynamic people on earth.

There are never many guests at The Wakaya Club and Spa. Fourteen couples is the maximum for a 2,200-acre property—an area that could, in the hands of other proprietors, be real estate enough for a population a hundred times greater. It's generously and graciously proportioned. The view of the Captain Bligh Strait and the distant islands is big; the tree-canopied hillside beyond the golf course is big; the South Pacific sky and the billowing, sun-shot clouds that roll in from the Koro Sea are big; the clear, star-splayed nights and the distant glimmering lights of Levuka, the ancient capital of Fiji, are big; the landscaped frontage—where white rope hammocks swing gently between coconut palms and where pairs of comfortable chaises look out to the water—is big.

But The Wakaya Club is also intimate, if you want it to be. You can meet your fellow guests at the bar of the Palm

Grove restaurant. Keith Richards was very comfortable there, sitting with Ronnie Wood and their wives, until the day of their now famous picnic. You can be sociable on the terrace or by the swimming pool if you choose. But if you want seclusion, the thatched-roof, seaside beach houses (known in Fijian as *bures*) are so widely spaced and so separated from one another by groves of ferns and flowers and tropical foliage, you can be entirely on your own. Wakaya is a place—both for our guests and for ourselves—that is as congenial or as private as we want it to be.

At Wakaya, Jill is uncompromising in her pursuit of excellence. It can be exhausting to get everything absolutely right. But here again, I think Jill's approach is one that is applicable to business. I can't tell you how often Jill has decided that something is just not quite good enough. She has a very keen eye, and the damnable thing is, invariably, she's right. But somehow her rigorous lack of compromise doesn't tire me out. Her sustained passion always makes me feel more enthusiastic, more idealistic, more hopeful.

One of the great joys of Wakaya is that I've found that I am more energized at the end of the process of designing, planning, and constructing a new building than I felt at the beginning. Certainly, my work on our agricultural programs is inspiring in exactly this way. I think it's because, in both instances, we keep reaching a little higher. We get closer to our unobtainable goal. Even as I write, Jill is redecorating each of the free-standing suites, and Russell Thornley is busy with our ginger paddocks and papaya groves. I know there are people who insist that spirituality can only exist in temple, or church, or synagogue, and that pleasure plays no role in such pursuits.

But I'm not buying. Humans delight in beauty. It speaks to our longing for things beyond the workaday, and beyond the compromises we have imposed on ourselves and on our environment. The combination of creative energy and natural splendour that is Wakaya produces—in me, at any rate—a peace of mind and a tranquility that I cherish.

Wakaya was a place my daughter Erin loved very much. We came here often for holidays, before the establishment of The Wakaya Club and Spa, when the island was one of the undeveloped holdings of Southern Pacific Hotels. When Erin was a little girl, it was a kind of magical desert island for her.

She loved everything about Fiji, and she especially loved the children. I used to call her the pied piper, because she seemed always to have a little gang of happy kids following her around.

Erin loved our holidays on Wakaya. They were special, for her and for me. It was a busy time in my life. My duties for Southern Pacific Hotels were racking up more air miles in a month than a reasonably well-travelled executive might log in a year in those days. Southern Pacific had developed a property called Pacific Harbour, and we were eager to follow up on its success. As Garth Hopkins wrote in the epilogue of his book on Clairtone, "David Gilmour spent much of the spring and summer of 1972 searching the world for that ideal site, and workable government/private sector combination that would produce another Pacific Harbour. The partners felt that they had proven the concept in Fiji and wanted to apply the formula again in another location."

During that time, I was far too often a postcard to Erin, or a long-distance call, or the handwriting on blue air-mail stationery, and far too seldom the father on a perfect holiday, strolling along a beautiful, otherwise empty beach, hand-in-hand with my delightful daughter. We made up for lost time on Wakaya.

The home Jill and I lived in for many years on Wakaya is called Vale-O. Our new home, Sega na Leqa, is much closer to the sea, but Vale-O is a hillside aerie. It has the view, so I often imagined, of a falcon, wings spread, poised on an updraft. From the high point of Vale-O I could see the lush, hillside canopy of trees below and the red roof of the village church in the distance—a quaint, old-fashioned-looking structure that Jill was very hands-on with and that we built for the employees and guests of The Wakaya Club and Spa. The multi-denominational church is the centrepiece of the village of 36 houses where our employees live, rent free and with no charge for their utilities. (Jill took great pride in designing the church, even importing lamps from Ovalau's sister island in the United States, Nantucket.) There is a school, a nursing station, a town hall, and a flood-lit playing field. The homes are comfortable and neatly kept. But it is the white-framed, red-roofed church that catches the eye from Vale-O.

The little church is very beautiful. The services are uplifting. The parishioners are warm and welcoming. Fijians are beautiful singers—never more beautiful than in a choir in church. Their faith is moving. Still, I seldom go. To be frank, it's too much for me. There is a stained-glass window there. It is an illustration of Christ with little children gathered round his feet. Suffer the little children. And one of the upturned faces is a likeness of my daughter.

A business philosophy we developed at Southern Pacific, and one I adhere to now, is that good fortune does not befall a company by accident. I believe it is a rule that has no exceptions. Unless, that is, you enjoy flirting with failure. Luck is where preparation meets opportunity. For example, in the early days of Southern Pacific we needed investors, and having spotted opportunity in our search, we did everything we could to prepare.

My friend, Jean-Georges Vongerichten—a man I consider to be one of the world's greatest chefs—has a similar philosophy. When asked about the secret of his success, he explains that great cooking is 70 percent ingredients and 30 percent talent. There are all kinds of businesses that could learn from Jean-Georges' advice. Somehow, it's something I took to heart early on in my career.

The hard work of my partners, Peter Munk and Bill Birchall, provided the essential ingredients to our presentations. I was the traveller of the team and the one designated to deliver our pitch. But whatever talent I brought to bear would have been for naught had the ingredients not been so thorough and so first class.

When Southern Pacific needed capital, we identified two investors we felt had interests that matched our own. I travelled to Hong Kong, and my trip had one purpose: to meet with Henry Keswick, executive chairman at Jardine Matheson. We met on a Thursday, and Henry asked me how long I'd be in Hong Kong. I replied, "As long as it will take you to make a decision." He pondered this. "Well, come by Monday. I need a little time to think."

A trip to London had the same purpose. My friends Lord "Gordy" White and Lord James Hanson introduced me to the man I wanted to meet, Jim Slater of Slater Walker Securities. I was confident no other door-knocking would be required.

In both instances, our presentations were very solid, very complete, and very specific. Peter Munk and Bill Birchall were very focused in this regard. We wanted Jardine Matheson and Slater Walker to know that there was nothing scattershot in our approach. We weren't guessing. We weren't hoping. We tailored our presentation very directly to the investors we had targeted. I returned from my travels with commitments from both. You could say, we got lucky—if, that is, you know what luck is.

It was 1974, a year I always think of as the Egypt year. Peter was in Australia. I was based in London. What had begun with a relatively modest acquisition of property in Fiji had been nurtured into a thriving hotel and resort chain throughout the South Pacific.

Long before Canadians began to hear of "the Pacific Rim" we were convinced that the South Pacific was about to undergo an enormous boom. And in this we proved to be correct. We had also formulated a plan that worked beautifully with the hotels, resorts, and hotel chains we were acquiring. And that, in essence, would later be our acquisition strategy with Barrick Gold. We bought individual companies, brought them together under a single umbrella, and created a management team from the best personnel to oversee the entire chain. In other words, as we would do later with gold mines, we created our own galaxy from the stars that we chose. We pooled talent, expertise, and resources. It proved to be an extraordinarily successful strategy.

The Egyptian Project grew directly from our experience with Southern Pacific. And, as has been the case with so many things, it all began at a dinner party.

I'd been invited to a dinner in London at the home of Charles Riachy, a well-known Lebanese businessman. Riachy was a bit of a rascal, a charming and notoriously successful womanizer. But he was highly regarded in the Middle-Eastern community of London. He was a bit of a scoundrel, but it was hard not to like him.

Among the guests at the dinner was Ashraf Marwan, the personal assistant to President Anwar Sadat of Egypt. He had married the daughter of President Nasser from the previous regime, and he was—so I could see immediately—a man of tremendous interest and intellect.

I asked Ashraf Marwan questions about Egypt and about Egyptian politics. I asked him about Sadat. I asked him about the challenges that Sadat's government faced and about what they hoped to accomplish. I listened more than I spoke.

He was taken, I think, with my curiosity. Indeed, this restraint on my part—the instinct to learn more about others than I reveal about myself—served me much better than had I set out to try to sell him on something. And anyway, from a business point of view, Egypt was about the last place on my mind. The focus of Southern Pacific Hotels was a world away—in Australia, in Hawaii, in Fiji, in Tahiti, in Japan, in New Zealand, in New Guinea.

He had asked me about my work, and I told him about Southern Pacific Hotels. I didn't go to great length, but I told him of my travels in search of sites for resort and hotel projects. I was, by then, spending a huge amount of time on airplanes. I told him we were a young and energetic company. I made it clear that we were also extremely ambitious.

He sized me up. Then, over the dinner table, he asked me what I was doing that coming weekend.

"Nothing," I replied.

He said, "Then please fly down. I want you to meet President Sadat and the minister of development and reconstruction, Osman Ahmed Osman."

I didn't need a lot of encouragement. I arrived in Cairo less than a week later. I was staying at the Sheraton Hotel on the Nile. I was in my room at about ten o'clock on my first night, and I got a call from Ashraf. He said, "We'll send a car around. I want you to come over to the Ministry and I'll introduce you."

Sadat's genius, like that of Ronald Reagan, was that he surrounded himself with brilliant, very high-calibre advisors. Osman was one of these. He was stocky and obviously strong. He was just as obviously enthusiastic. I'd go so far as to say that an energy emanated from him. I sensed it as soon as I walked into his office.

He'd been responsible for Egypt's biggest project, at least the biggest since the Pyramids. He had masterminded the Aswan Dam, an engineering miracle. But a miracle of project management and strategy as well. Many bureaucratic and political quagmires lurked behind the smiling faces of mid-level Egyptian bureaucrats. I'd learn that soon enough.

Osman, like Sadat, had huge aspirations for Egypt. He tended to think big, and it was perfectly clear that I was not there to discuss anything modest. It was also quickly obvious to me that my Egyptian trip was not going to involve sitting around on pillows sipping sweet tea and smoking hookahs. This was a government desperately keen to switch into high gear. Sadat was intent on revolutionizing his country—wrenching it, if necessary, into the modern era—and his ambition was certainly apparent in the upper reaches of the government and the civil service. These guys weren't fooling around. They were working furiously to overcome the paralysis of indecision that Nasser's socialism had bequeathed to an entire generation. When I arrived at the Ministry at one o'clock in the morning, there was Osman Ahmed Osman at his desk.

We spoke in a general way about tourism and about the possibilities of development in Egypt. I felt the greatest admiration for Osman's intellect and curiosity. And there was no doubt that we had the attention of the very top of the Egyptian government. The next day, I met President Sadat.

Sadat welcomed me with a dignity that was no less warm because it was so statesman-like. He had a phenomenal presence. His aura, one of power and confidence, became the focal point of any room in which he stood. I liked him immensely. He was a visionary, and a true Egyptian patriot.

Sadat explained to me that his hope was to establish a tourist destination in Egypt that would bring in five million tourists a year. I appreciated the scope of the ambition. And I had no doubt that Egypt had enormous untapped potential for tourism. But I countered with a slightly different approach. With all due respect, I offered another point of view.

I knew what lay ahead. "Don't go for numbers," I said. "Because then you get pollution of the airports, of the culture, of the cities. If you bring in the lowest end of tourism, in the greatest possible numbers, you begin to undermine the value of what you have. Why not think about cutting that number by three-quarters and aiming at the top end of the tourism industry. You'll attract further foreign investment with this approach to tourism. As well as the investment in bricks and mortar, you'll be investing in the unique experience of Egypt. Bring in people who won't just come for five days, but who will stay for a serious period of time and therefore really contribute to the economy of Egypt."

Sadat considered this. Then he nodded. He liked this approach. So did his advisors.

We were invited to make a proposal. The Egyptian government would provide 10,000 hectares of land on the Giza Plateau. We would provide the concept, the design, the construction plan, and the financing. This development would be one of the largest travel destinations in the world, and when it was complete, there would be a further 10,000 hectares on the Egyptian coast near the Libyan border to be developed. Following my meeting, I was on the first flight I could book.

Peter and I, and our associates at Southern Pacific, brainstormed and debated, and gradually focused on a plan for the 10,000-hectare site, close by the pyramids, on the high plateau in the desert. The Pyramid Oasis was perfect, and perfectly respectful of its environs. If we kept our development low-rise, nothing over 60 feet high, the resort would be able to see the pyramids, but the pyramids would be unable to see the resort.

We brought in Robert Trent Jones, Jr., the famous golf course architect, and he designed a beautiful course in the shape of an ankh. Then, through Mark McCormack at International Management Group—the man who would be best man at Jill's and my wedding—we contacted Bjorn Borg, one of the best tennis players in the world at that time. We'd have a Bjorn Borg tennis camp. We'd have a Trent Jones golf course. We would create a place beautifully and sensitively designed to which people would come for extended luxury stays.

Peter and I returned to Egypt with our plans, and we were both having trouble containing our excitement. The Pyramid Oasis felt a long way from a beleaguered electronics plant in Nova Scotia.

Peter and I don't always agree on everything. Sometimes, I've noticed, our memories of certain events in our past are not entirely in synch. But on this, we are both in absolute agreement. Presenting our proposal to the President of Egypt was an extraordinary moment.

We were ushered into the Egyptian throne room—a space of grand, even intimidating, formality. Sadat greeted us with a smile of calm equanimity. I had the maps, plans, and architectural renderings of our plan rolled beneath my arm. We spoke for a while, answering Sadat's perceptive questions, and upon his request to see our plans, I began to open them up for his inspection. President Sadat was curious to see what we had come up with—so curious that he suggested that we discuss the plans in positions much more practical and altogether less formal than the kind of posture normally seen in the throne room. Like many great men, he was not one to stand on ceremony. There are few things that Peter and I value more than the photograph that was taken that day of Peter Munk, David Gilmour, and Anwar Sadat—on our hands and knees on the beautiful carpet of the Egyptian throne room as we looked over our plans.

President Sadat very much liked what he saw that day. Our

plans for the Pyramid Oasis suited his ambitions for his country. It was my great good fortune to meet with this distinguished statesman on several occasions after that.

After our throne room meeting, Sadat and his minister of tourism said that they would sign the deal on my next trip to Egypt. I think that this proposal was intentionally vague—made in the spirit of the elasticity of time that prevails in the Middle East: There is no reason to make a decision today if it can be made tomorrow. But neither Peter nor I wanted to lose our momentum. And so we took the Egyptians at their word.

That period was among the busiest of my periodic bursts of frenzied travel. I got on a flight from Cairo to Japan to meet with contractors. Then I flew to Los Angeles for a few meetings. Then to London. And then back to Cairo. Our Egyptian associates were surprised when, ten days after I'd last seen them, I was back at their offices. They didn't realize that I had even left.

"But we said we would sign on your next trip to Egypt," they exclaimed.

"I've been around the world," I replied. "And, as you can see, I am back."

I think they realized then that we were serious.

Alas, the project—so promising and so full of so many potential benefits—was sunk by an intransigent bureaucracy, by the vested interests of a leftist elite, by criminals, and by fundamentalists who were only too happy to see Egypt sink back into the Middle Ages. Had the Pyramid Oasis project been completed, it would have been the largest contributor to the economy and the largest single employer in Egypt. But such practical concerns were of little interest to the fanatics and ideologues who opposed us.

The communists were only too happy to sabotage the plans of the infidel foreigners, and eventually I came to realize that there was good reason to be concerned for my own safety. I was advised that there were at least three factions in Cairo that would be more than happy to be rid of me—quite an uncomfortable feeling, and one that inspired me to revise my will with Jill's future in mind should anything untoward happen. I remember how strange it was describing this unsettling reality to disbelieving friends. "It's the sort of thing," I said, "that, in Chicago, in the old days, was called a contract." For the first time in my life, I had a bodyguard—however the fact that he was most often found sleeping in the doorway of my hotel did not give me the greatest comfort. I also, for the first time, had a driver, named Mohammed. After an accident on our way to meet with President Sadat one day, I was advised by the President to tell Mohammed in no uncertain terms, "Please slow down, I am in a hurry."

It was a period of considerable unrest—early troubling signs of the divisions we see today between Muslim fundamentalists and the Western world. There were riots in Cairo—fire bombs, overturned buses—and it became untenable for Sadat to continue with a project that appeared to be so pro-Western.

President Sadat got word to us that because of the political turmoil he would have to cancel the project. He told us that he was sickened by this, but that he had decided that he would have to offer the carrot of cancelling the Pyramid Oasis project to his troublesome opponents. Sadat, it was clear to us, was picking his battles. And even though the news was distressing in the extreme, I could see that it was politically wise. Sadat was obliged to play a cunning game, all the more so because so many forces aligned against him came from inside the country's mid-management and his own civil service. But somewhere—over the heads of the intransigent bureaucrats and religious zealots— somewhere in the distance, he could see where Egypt needed to go. It was a dream of democracy and education and prosperity that I believe has fuelled the recent astonishing events in North Africa and in the Middle East.

Sadat was, in this way, a great idealist. But he was also a very practical man, and he knew how much attaining his goal would depend on compromise, strategic alliances, diplomacy and the willingness to make unpalatable decisions. The demise of the Pyramid Oasis was such a decision, alas.

But not even political wisdom can see the future. On October 6, 1981, that gracious and far-sighted man who had so welcomed us was assassinated by the same dark, backward-looking forces that he was dedicated to overcoming. He had made the mistake of reaching. His sin had been wanting to excel.

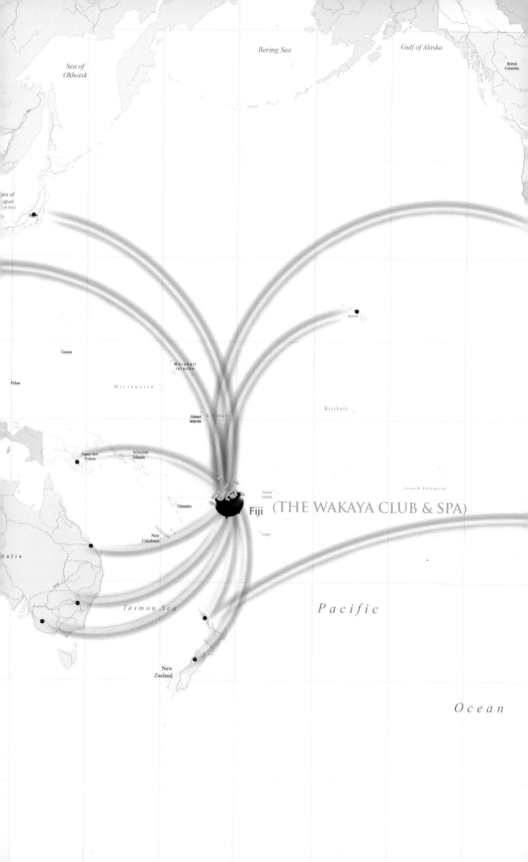

A MARVELOUS PARTY

"It is my belief, you cannot deal with the most serious things in the world unless you understand the most amusing."
—Sir Winston Churchill

IF EVER YOU GET THE URGE TO OPEN A RESTAURANT, my advice is that you lie down until the feeling goes away.

Restaurants are a demanding, nerve-jangling, headache-inspiring, unforgiving business—one that amateurs should keep clear of at all costs. There are less painful, less exhausting, less stressful, and less heart-breaking ways to lose sleep and money.

The best chefs and the most experienced owners admit that running a restaurant often takes a terrible toll—on one's psyche, on one's physical energies, on one's ego, as well as on one's bank account. For a businessman like me, someone who likes to leave nothing to chance, there are just too many variables and too many potential disasters-in-waiting in the restaurant business. If you don't know what you're doing, and most people don't, you'll probably be happier banging your head against a wall.

There are, however, exceptions that prove every rule. And Drones, the restaurant that some friends and I opened in London in the 1970s, was exactly that. It was a kind of miracle.

I'd had some related experience in this kind of a business before. I was a director of Le Club, America's first discotheque, in the 1960s. Le Club was in New York City and it was a mecca for international society. It was instructive for me, and enormous fun, to be involved with "the hippest place to be" for the most fascinating people in the world. Still, my experience at Le Club (I later became chairman in the 1980s) was nothing like the hands-on start-up of Drones.

Against all odds it was as much fun to run Drones as we (naïvely) imagined it would be when we conceived of the idea. From its very first night until the day we sold it ten years later, it was an endlessly amusing adjunct to my London life.

Well, perhaps not endlessly amusing …

One of the unexpected results of Drones' success was that until I got an unlisted number, my phone rang day and night. My low celebrity profile had led hurried journalists to jump to the conclusion that David Gilmour, rock star, was the David Gilmour of Drones.

I have lived in 16 homes since my time in London, but I still keep an unlisted number. As a result, I sleep much better than I used to when the phone rang at all hours. I like to say that it was far too exhausting entertaining all those beautiful young women who wanted to come around in the middle of the night to talk to me about Pink Floyd, but for some reason Jill finds this less amusing than I do.

Drones became an institution—a meeting place of London's most elegant, most successful, most colourful, and most interesting people. I can see it vividly still in my mind's eye: the white and black harlequin floor; the hanging, galvanized buckets full of scarlet geraniums, the framed early American quilts; the natural light spilling from on high through the building's original atrium, the stained-glass window that rose, up the stairwell, from the lower level to the ceiling, diffusing a kind of magic over everything. There was a small dining area on the lower floor—a corner of the restaurant that we referred to affectionately as Siberia because it was not where our regular customers were ever seated, unless, of course, some cad was there with someone he shouldn't have been with and preferred not to be seen at all. Drones' candy-twist Victorian furniture was painted all white, as if in a set designed by Cecil Beaton.

Drones had a distinctly London hubbub that I remember so well. The pop stars and the actors, the crooks and the politicians, the aristocrats and the Hollywood producers, the models there after their bookings, and the real estate brokers there after the models. The place was pulsing with London's life.

I can see Luis, the maître d'. We had stolen him from Tramps, a recruitment that was not particularly underhanded.

Tramps was the most popular private dining and disco club in London, run by our friends Johnny Gold and Jackie Collins' husband, Oscar Lerman. But hiring personnel away from existing institutions is a way of life in the restaurant world. It's just the way things are done. After all, where else are you going to find a good, experienced maître d'? It's not as if they are waiting around at the labour exchange. A good maître d'hôtel is worth his weight in gold—and therefore is almost never without a job.

There's Luis, in my mind's eye, guiding Jimmy Goldsmith to his table at Drones while at the bar, one of the two bartenders we'd stolen from the American Bar at the Connaught is mixing a cocktail for Tony Curtis, or Peter O'Toole, or Dudley Moore, or Annabelle Churchill, or George Hamilton, or Roman Polanski.

As P.T. Barnum once put it: "Nothing draws a crowd like a crowd." And at Drones, every night, we certainly had a crowd. As a matter of fact, we had the crowd. We brought together the ingredients, and mixed the perfect cocktail. As the famous Noël Coward song goes, it was "a marvelous party."

It all started one Friday night in 1972 at my London home. My gang of friends included David Niven, Jr., the managing director of Columbia Pictures; Kirk Kerkorian, the owner of MGM; the well-known Lebanese businessman Charles Riachy; Nickey Kerman, Roger Moore, Jack Weiner, the film director; David Frost, Lord (Gordy) White, and various business associates. We often celebrated the end of the week with cocktails and convivial conversation, and that night, as some of us were chatting, an idea began to form. A seed was planted that Niven and I later brought to fruition.

These were my bachelor days. Erin's mother and I were

divorced. It would be some years before Jill would walk into my life. So I was footloose and fancy free in London—and there were few cities in the world more amenable to the plight of the lonely, fun-loving bachelor than London was in those days.

I had moved from New York City better to carry out my Southern Pacific duties. Two of our principal shareholders, P&O Shipping and Trusthouse Forte, were London-based companies, and so a London address made more sense than Toronto or New York. I was the road warrior of my Southern Pacific partnership with my friends, Peter Munk and Bill Birchall, largely because I'd never lost my wanderlust. I was appointed the designated traveller, the man dispatched on company business to Fiji, Sydney, Singapore, Hong Kong, and Tokyo. London was a convenient home base for my many necessary trips.

And there was another reason, I admit, for my London residency: I've always loved that great city. I have many friends there. I love its beautiful parks and magnificent buildings. I was always as intrigued with cab drivers and fishmongers as I was by aristocrats and celebrities. The colourful locals in the pub are as entertaining to me as the swells at Ascot.

London suited me to the ground. I had a lovely home on Eaton Square. To quote from that same Noël Coward song, "I couldn't have liked it more."

On the Friday evening when we stumbled onto the idea for Drones, my friends and I were engaged in trying to solve a vexing problem. Where were we going to go to kick off the weekend?

The problem we immediately confronted was the eclectic variety of our dress. At that time, London society still clung to strictly regimented dress codes, but from a practical point of view it was very difficult to adhere to them. Gone were the days when a group of men, gathering after work, would all be dressed with identical formality. Some of my friends that evening were in business suits. One, having just returned from Pinewood Studios, was in jeans, and one, planning to attend a charity event later in the evening, was in black tie. Uniform we were not.

Over our cocktails, we remarked on this dilemma. Where could we all go together, dressed so variously, other than a pub? It was a conundrum peculiar to London. And as we discussed our problem we all noted, with some chagrin, that in New York, a group of friends in jeans, business suits, and black tie would not have presented difficulties. PJ Clarke's was a popular New York restaurant that had made its name with simple but excellent fare, and a casually flexible approach to dress that reflected the changing fashions of the day.

Things were very different in London. You got dressed, and dressed very properly, if you were going out for the evening—whether to a private club, or to a social event, or to dine at the Connaught Grill Room, or the Ritz, or the dining room at Claridge's. London maître d's were famously unbending on these regulations. Once, the famous designer Oleg Cassini and I were almost denied entry to Annabel's, the private restaurant and nightclub on Berkeley Square, because Oleg was wearing a very elegant midnight blue suit. It was hand-stitched. It was beautifully tailored. I have no doubt that it was more expensive than most of the dinner jackets that sailed past us as we stood at the door arguing with the maître d'. But Annabel's had a no blue jean rule that was not to be taken lightly. And Oleg's suit happened to be made of very fine denim. Oh, the horror!

The dilemma of the friends who had gathered at my home on Eaton Square that night in 1972 was hardly the end of the world. We were going to find a way to enjoy ourselves one way or another. But as we joked about London society's quaint inflexibility, we stumbled onto a truth that became more and more intriguing the more we explored it. The place we wanted to go—elegant, hip, and amusing—did not exist. There was no place where Mick Jagger, in jeans, could sit with Lord Snowdon, in black tie, with Jean Shrimpton, in a miniskirt, with Princess Margaret in an evening gown.

Conception, of course, is never the difficult part. What follows the act of conceiving is usually less resplendent with delight. But from the outset, Drones seemed an idea blessed with good fortune. Its labour—eight months of renovation and decoration—went more smoothly than anyone would have imagined possible. Even its birth was so easy, so painless, and so generally fortuitous that we quickly became the envy of club owners and restaurateurs throughout the city. What was our secret? I was asked again and again. I'm not really sure I knew the answer—other than to say that we followed our instincts. There was no place to go one Friday evening. So we thought we'd dream one up.

I was born in Winnipeg, Manitoba, Canada, in 1931. How my

mother ever spoke to me again after putting up with a 10-month pregnancy and my 12-pound entry into the world, I'll never know.

She was a very strong woman. She had to be. As well as the mother of four children and a glamorous and loving wife, she was an opera singer. And I don't mean she was a housewife who liked to sing opera. She was the real thing: beautiful, dramatic, and passionate about her art. It is perhaps from my mother that I inherited the conviction with which I throw myself into my enterprises. When she took on a role, she took on a role. The title role in *Tosca*, Santuzza in *Cavalleria Rusticana*, Elizabeth in *Tannhäuser*, and Elsa in *Lohengrin*—all were in her repertoire.

I had three doting sisters. They were six, eight and twelve years old when I was born—making me, perhaps, a bit of an afterthought. I'm told that our home was large and comfortable, with a pleasant garden, on Gertrude Avenue in Winnipeg, but my memories of that period are little more than pleasantly vague dreams, augmented, probably, by stories I heard and photographs I saw later in my life.

That happy household was where I spent the first two years of my life. Dad was manager of the Winnipeg Grain Exchange. He had returned from the First World War and met my mother, the beautiful daughter of an English colonel. My grandfather was visiting Canada from London, via the Natal Rebellion and the First World War. Such was the itinerant life of a professional soldier in those days.

My grandfather eventually became Provost-Marshal for Canada, and my mother often remarked that he had survived

Zulu spears in South Africa and the trenches of Flanders only to put his life more seriously at risk in Canada. As Provost-Marshal, he was an outspoken proponent of conscription, a position that, so Mother maintained, made him a target more than once when he was touring Quebec.

Mother cut a very striking figure, and nobody was more struck than Dad. He first set eyes on her in Fort Gary on Christmas in 1921. By all accounts, he fell in love with her on the spot. He was a war hero, as dashing as Mother was beautiful.

They had a long and happy marriage, though one that apparently began with more passion than was considered prudent in their day. There was a very heavy snowstorm in Fort Gary when they met. People were socked-in for days, a turn of events that apparently quite suited Mother and Father. I eventually figured out that my oldest sister's birthdate does not quite jive (in the proper, old-fashioned sense) with the date of our parents' wedding.

We moved to Toronto in 1933 when I was two. Dad had been appointed Managing Director for Ontario operations of the Canadian stock brokerage firm Nesbitt, Thomson. Mother, who had trained at the London Conservatory, and had sung with the Winnipeg Symphony Orchestra, continued her career as an opera singer. I have vivid memories of listening to her beautiful voice echoing through the house as she practiced.

Our house was the centre of my parents' active social life. When I was a boy I used to peer down from the minstrel gallery of our family home on Oriole Parkway and spy on my parents' parties. I was always fascinated. On one side of the living room were Father's well-heeled business and sporting friends, and on the other side were Mother's colourful and frequently penniless artistic crowd. You could draw a line between the two, although the two worlds met in the remarkable marriage of my parents.

I was lucky in this regard. Because, the truth is, the dividing line that I could see in my parents' living room continues in life—and, thanks to my upbringing, I've always tried to ignore it. Dividing lines are never useful to the entrepreneur.

I learned long ago that the best advice often comes from unlikely sources. Here's a recent example: "The lights have gone out," is how a young Latino man described to me the changes that the new owners of FIJI Water have made to the bottle we originally designed. I was shopping in Whole Foods in New York at the time, and there on the shelf before us were six bottles of the original FIJI Water bottle, and six of the new design, and, yes, it was perfectly clear: The lights had gone out. But no one had quite stated this fact with the clarity of that young man.

That the young man is a clerk at Whole Foods, and not a highly-paid marketing consultant, doesn't make his observation something to be taken lightly. His opinion, unsolicited and honest, is more instructive to me than that of a dozen focus groups. My advice is always to listen to the people on the front lines. The best generals are the ones who pay attention to the folks in the trenches.

Ideas come from all quarters. Indeed, some of the most important positions in the companies I've owned have been held by people I've hired from outside the industry into which I was entering. It's a policy of mine.

I'm always looking for a new and original perspective, and new and original are not usually the chief characteristics of someone who has spent a good part of a career within the confines of a single industry. I am a businessman, but there is no reason why my ideas should come to me exclusively from the business world. My advice to budding entrepreneurs everywhere is simply this: Do your best to cross the dividing lines.

One of the people I believe who does this best is also one of my newer friends and colleagues, David M. Roth, one of my estate's trustees who has taken the reins of many of my business ventures and manages many of my personal assets. David and I first met in Fiji and spent the better part of five hours over dinner talking about a range of diverse subjects, from religion and politics to opera, wine, books, and technology—and it seems we have not stopped talking since. David has a world of experience in places such as Namibia, Ethiopia, Palau, Micronesia, and Tonga. He is as well known in Washington, D.C., as he is in the Pacific (he was the proud recipient of the Order of the Crown, an honour bestowed on him by the late King George Tupou V), and is one of those rare people with whom I have developed a deep and significant connection that is sure to pass the test of time. David knows how to effectively cross the dividing lines that too often separate us from the very best ideas.

Instincts aren't hocus-pocus. They are our brains processing a whole myriad of signals about a person, and many of the signals are subtle, complex, and beneath the radar of the simple categorization that is the language of the résumé. To have the nerve to "go with your gut" is one of those things that is much easier said than done—but, in my view, it is an invaluable tool in business.

When I was growing up, Toronto was still an outpost of the Empire. Stiff upper lip. Scotch and soda. Membership at the Badminton and Racquet Club, the Granite Club, the Royal Canadian Yacht Club. An account at T. Eaton Company and the Robert Simpson Company. A pew at Grace Church on the Hill, or St. James, or St. Paul's, or St. Simeon. Toronto's establishment sang "God Save the King" with gusto, ate roast beef and Yorkshire pudding on Sundays, and celebrated Queen Victoria's birthday on the 24th of May.

As was the colonial way, Toronto spent a good deal more time and energy thinking about Britain than Britain ever spent thinking about it. This imperial indifference did nothing to reduce the city's fervent loyalty to the Crown. There were cannons from the Crimean War in front of the provincial legislature and an equestrian statue of King Edward VII behind it. I was brought up in a place where the Union Jack flew from every flagpole and where everything came to a stop on Christmas morning when we all listened to the royal message from Buckingham Palace.

Even so, as traditionally English as my upbringing had been, little of my life had prepared me for the harsh reality of the Canadian version of an old-fashioned English boarding school. I went from being pampered by a mother and three sisters to a grim world of caning and quarters and study halls and fagging. Nothing in my past had braced me for the cold, draughty corridors, for the windswept playing fields, for the cruelty of the bullies I encountered there. Or for my nickname.

During the first half of my first year at boarding school, I was called Lily. As you can imagine, it wasn't a nickname I cared for very much. But there's a kind of collective genius to boarding school nicknames. Often they capture some cruel truth. And the fact is I was tall, fair-haired, skinny, and pale. Lily was not off the mark.

I was 13. I had been pushed forward a grade in order to get into the boarding school my parents had decided on for me. I was the youngest boy in the senior school in my first year. Suddenly, I was in a strange place, surrounded by people I did not know.

In those days, boxing was one of the obligatory athletic activities at the school. I had never boxed before. I had no idea what to do in a ring, really, although I'd seen pictures and boxing scenes in movies, I suppose. And so I was less than thrilled when the gym teacher announced that I would be paired against one of the bigger boys in the class. Worse yet, he was one of the bullies who had been tormenting me. "Oh good," my opponent declared ominously. "I get Lily."

I climbed into the ring. My schoolmates gathered round, intent on seeing how quickly I'd end up on the canvas. I remember feeling at first as if my knees might give out.

I crouched and bobbed, feinted and weaved, and generally did the best that I could to stay out of harm's way. But there are not a lot of places to hide in a boxing ring, and eventually I was obliged to engage, as best I could, with my much bigger and much more experienced opponent.

I remember holding my gloves up in front of my face, trying to protect myself. This was effective, defensively speaking. As an offensive strategy, however, it was without a great deal of promise.

Free of any danger of counter-punches, my opponent pummeled me without restraint. It appeared as if I were incapable of retaliation. As a result, he let his guard drop. I don't think he was taunting me. He just felt he could get away with being careless. Big mistake.

Suddenly, as if it were acting on its own accord, my right fist shot through the air. It was a real, old-fashioned haymaker, and I can still see my own glove flying past my head on its way to his. I think it surprised me nearly as much as it surprised him.

The next thing I knew he was flat on the canvas. My classmates were cheering. Lily, indeed. To this day I'm not sure where that roundhouse right came from. Instinct, I suppose.

Finding the right site for a restaurant—the right combination of an appropriate space and the right address—is all about instinct. And it's notoriously difficult.

This was especially true in a city in which fashion was as changeable and real estate as much in demand as London. But once again, the gods smiled. Number One Pont Street was only two blocks from where I lived, and on my first outing as our location scout, Number One Pont Street was as far as my search for the perfect site for Drones took me.

It was an antique store—long, spacious, high-ceilinged— that was definitely big enough for our purposes. As well, it happened to be filled with exactly the furniture and curios that we needed for the interior we envisioned. And, best of all, it was a store owned and run by two charming gentlemen who were reaching the age at which selling the business and enjoying retirement in Spain was looking more and more attractive.

I explained our plans and asked them, should they be interested in selling their lease, to come up with a figure. If their price was not one we could afford, I'd wish them well and be on my way. I had no interest in embarking on a protracted game of low-ball, high-ball that might never be resolved.

They pondered this for a day or two, and got back with a price that, with no further bartering, accorded with our budget. Suddenly—effortlessly, it seemed—we were underway.

The name we had chosen—Drones—was the name of Bertie Wooster's fictitious club in P.G. Wodehouse's delightful comic novels. And it was Niven who undertook to write Wodehouse a letter, requesting his permission for us to use it. This wasn't strictly a legal obligation, but part of Niven's charm was his consideration. As he made clear, it was the gentlemanly thing to do.

Wodehouse entered entirely into the spirit of things. Demonstrating both an enthusiasm for our enterprise and a familiarity with the local geography, he pointed out that Drones was the perfect name for what we had in mind, as it was next door to a dry-cleaners called Jeeves. The letter from P.G. Wodehouse was promptly framed, to be hung in a place of honour in our new restaurant.

Our budget for interior design was, shall I say, limited. None of us wanted to take this undertaking too, too seriously. None of us wanted something that had started out as a bit of a giggle to become an enormous investment. But more importantly, I had a hunch that mahogany and brass, heavy-framed Tissot engravings, and yards of Colefax & Fowler fabric was not the way to go. My instincts told me that London was ready for a place that was clever and fun. A spot that was chic but in an amusing way, stylish but in a manner that was possessed of a certain casual elegance and a certain sense of humour.

The curios that we acquired with our site were hardly fine antiques, which was perfect for us. When painted white they brought an element of wit and whimsy to Drones that quickly became its essential personality. Early American quilts were framed on white trellises and hung throughout the interior, acting as both acoustic baffles and a suitably idiosyncratic element of the Drones look.

Our next step, if I may say, was a stroke of genius. Niven had enviable contacts in the entertainment world, and he put them to good use on our behalf. Over his signature, we wrote to

150 celebrities and asked them to send a baby picture of themselves. Grace Kelly, Cary Grant, Ava Gardner, Clint Eastwood, Elizabeth Taylor, Robert Wagner, Lauren Bacall—all were among those who sent us photographs. Tony Curtis had no baby pictures, but sent us a picture of himself in his Brooklyn Sea Scout uniform. The Queen Mother didn't send a picture, but she did send us a note which, like the letter from the creator of Bertie Wooster and Jeeves, was framed and put on prominent display. Golda Meir wished us well but claimed that cameras had not yet been invented when she was born. One of the pictures—of a gentleman I am too discreet to name—was a nude baby shot that led several of the female habitués to note that not much had changed since it had been taken. The photographs were enlarged by friends of ours at *Vogue* magazine, and they constituted what must surely have been the least expensive and most talked-about décor in London.

Nor could we go wrong with our opening. It was as if the Fates had opened a publicity firm and had taken us on as their only clients.

Not that we wanted to make the evening of our launch a big event. Drones opened a scant eight months after our plan was set into motion, and it seemed suddenly that the first night was upon us. We had all attended too many hysterical opening nights to relish the prospect of such hoopla. Typically, restaurant or club openings were crowded, smoke-filled affairs that featured both slow service and an inability to see any of a new establishment's decorative details. So we decided to avoid such nonsense and have a "soft opening"—a chance to invite only our friends and families to Drones' inauguration. Our intention was twofold: to celebrate our first night and to test run the staff and the kitchen.

But word got out. Despite the fact that our opening was by invitation only, a line-up materialized at the door. A line-up, of course, is a good thing. You want a restaurant to have a line-up on its first night. But it wasn't a very good thing if you happened to be in that particular line-up, on that particular night, for the simple reason that the line wasn't going anywhere. Our restaurant was filled to capacity with our invitees, all of whom were having a delightful time. There was, alas, no way to allow anyone into the establishment without asking someone already inside to leave. And nobody was leaving such a good party.

Luis, our maître d', had to explain this over and over to the hopefuls gathered at our door. One young man was becoming particularly insistent about getting in, but as Luis had no intention of asking anyone to leave, he was regretful but equally insistent in his response. As it happened, Nigel Dempster, the celebrated gossip columnist—or, as he preferred it, "the *Daily Mail*'s resident social diarist"—was standing directly behind the young man. Dempster was a colourful, high-profile denizen of Fleet Street—the journalist who more or less created the modern gossip column—and the fact that Dempster was waiting in line was indicative of the remarkable word-of-mouth that attended our opening. But it was what Dempster wrote about the persistent young man that really put us on the map. His headline the next day was "Prince Charles Turned Away at Drones." We were so hot that not even the Prince of Wales could get in. Our reputation was made.

There was no looking back. Drones became the place to

be seen. Whether at the bar or in the dining area, on most nights you could see people in white tie on their way to the opera, actors and musicians in jeans and open-necked shirts, models and art directors, merchant bankers and industrialists, MPs and advertising executives. Because I lived so close at hand and because I was a bachelor, I was there four or five times a week to have dinner or lunch, or to meet with friends, or just to watch the passing scene. It was endlessly fascinating. Anyone of interest who was in London ended up at Drones. It was as if the world passed through my own local canteen. Before long, Hollywood producers, when planning a trip to the U.K., would make reservations a month in advance in order to avoid disappointment.

Almost immediately, it took on an iconic status—as if it were an institution that had been established for decades. I have a very vivid memory of Richard Harris—drunk, as usual—rudely abusing my friends, Lords Hanson and White. They were trying to enjoy their aperitifs with my friend and fellow Drones owner, David Niven, Jr.

Drunk and belligerent was not an unusual condition for Richard, I'm afraid, but on the occasion I recall, one of our most faithful clients, the famous gangster Reggie Kray, decided that he had heard enough. Reggie sidled over to Niven, and asked if he'd like Harris taken care of. Niven demurred. To which Reggie protested, couldn't he at least "break 'is legs"?

On another occasion I was at Annabel's, late at night, with a date, when a very pretty young woman approached me in floods of tears. She turned out to be the daughter of the actress Patricia Neal and she told me that there had been a terrible fire at Drones.

Had I heard? I had not.

As it turned out, it had been a flash fire in the kitchen. One in which, thankfully, nobody was hurt and that, while it did some damage, was not a major setback. Still, the young woman who approached me at Annabel's seemed almost inconsolable. Having seen the smoke and the fire trucks when she passed Drones earlier in the evening, she clung to me as if the worst possible calamity had befallen us both. I said how fortunate it was that nobody had been injured. And I tried to comfort what seemed to me to be a display of grief beyond what might customarily be inspired by a grease fire in a kitchen. I suppose my bemusement was apparent. "But Mr. Gilmour," she said, "you don't understand. I was taken out to dinner at Drones the night I lost my virginity." Clearly, our restaurant had entered into London mythology.

It was a place where people were thrown together in unlikely proximity, sometimes with surprising results. Niven once overheard a couple of sharply dressed but heavy-looking characters at the bar. Clearly they were trying to shake down Luis for protection money. Niven calmly intervened. He proposed a walk around the square.

As they strolled, Niven pointed out to the two would-be extortionists that "a certain family" with which they were sure to be familiar were among our regular clientele. There wasn't much doubt about who that family was.

Niven has a knack for establishing improbable friendships, and somehow had come to be on friendly terms with the elderly mother of the Kray brothers. The Krays were notorious East End gangsters. Reggie, in particular, was fond of Drones.

Niven went on to mention to his two strolling companions—in an entirely pleasant, unthreatening, conversational manner—that Vic Gilbert, Head of Special Branch, Scotland Yard, was also someone who was frequently at our bar and in our dining room.

The two thugs got the point. They were never heard from again.

And on it went—for five sittings a day, seven days a week, for almost ten years. It's a period of my life that I think of as one of the busiest (Southern Pacific Hotels was growing rapidly) and one of the most amusing. But all good things must come to an end, even, sometimes, when the wind of success is still in your sails. Work—my real work, that is—took me away from London.

There are not many businesses that can be run successfully by long distance, but this is particularly true of a restaurant. Unable to retain a regular presence, I sold Drones when I moved back to North America, but I was sad to close that chapter of my life. The new owner made the mistake that is often made in business. In order to put his fingerprints on his acquisition, he set out to fix what, most definitely, was not broken. Down came the baby pictures, up went tasteless paintings that were sold off the wall. Corners were cut, the buzz steadily diminished, and under its new owners, our beloved Drones ground to its inevitable halt. Eventually, the name was purchased by another restaurant group.

Apparently, many men fantasize about someday running a saloon and owning an island. I've done both—very happily.

The year we opened Drones, 1972, was also the year I first saw the island of Wakaya. And while my involvement with Drones seemed a departure, in a way it was an indication of what was to come. Drones was the creation of exactly what a group of friends wanted—a chic, casual gathering place for interesting and amusing people.

Years later, The Wakaya Club and Spa had the same kind of origin. Jill and I saw something that needed to be created. And we created it. We still are creating it. We trusted our instincts—and, as things have turned out, our instincts have served us well—like that boxing glove, sailing past my startled gaze, on its way toward success.

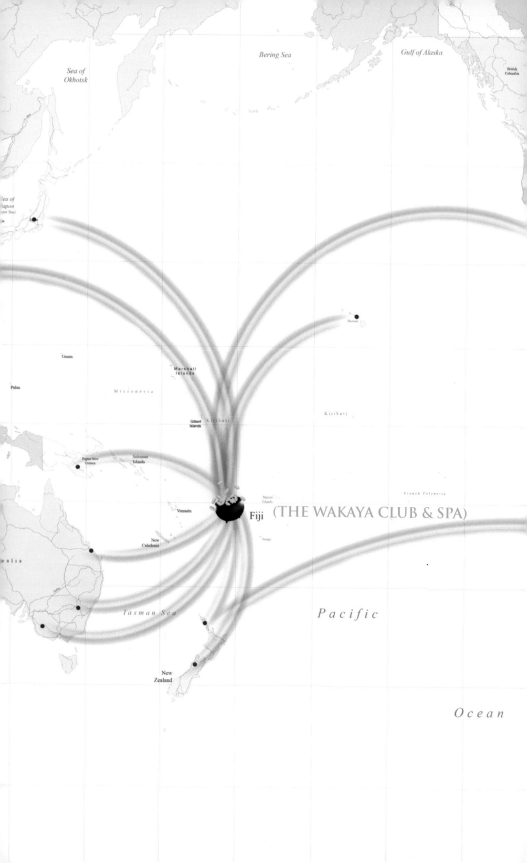

THE DESCENT

"If you are going through hell, keep going."
—Sir Winston Churchill

ON THE NIGHT OF THE DECEMBER SOLSTICE, 1983,
the weather had turned cool and blustery. Had you stood in front
of our home, a couple of hours after midnight, I doubt that you
would have seen a single light on in any of the comfortable, well-
tended houses on the gently curving streets of Lyford Cay. Before
the phone rang, the only sound was the dry rustle of the palms
outside our bedroom window. In winter, in the Caribbean, darkness falls suddenly.

Jill's and my life in the Bahamas was easy-going and tranquil. This suited me at the time. I can see now that there was
an element of limbo to it. I was between things, which is not
really a place I like to be. Nothing makes me happier than being
immersed in a new project. But even for a restless soul there are
times when it is necessary to take stock. Nassau was a restorative
interlude after what had been a busy period of my life. It had been
a while since I'd had a chance to catch my breath.

It was pleasant to wake up each day and not have to think

for a moment: Where am I? London? Cairo? Sydney? Until Jill and I had decided to give ourselves a break, my days had often been about wake-up calls, airports, and business meetings. Now our days were filled with reading, with tennis, with the beach, with luncheons with friends, with house guests—but mostly with making plans for our future.

I was 52. I was successful and healthy. I was in love. I was blessed with a beautiful wife, many good friends, and the most wonderful daughter a father could hope for. I was shifting my attention away from Southern Pacific Hotels and looking beyond. The days ahead were filled with what, to me, is one of the most exciting words in the English language: possibility.

The night breeze from the sea was soft and cool. The air was fresh, and Jill and I were both sleeping soundly. Our two dachshunds, Monte and Carlo, were in their basket. Above us, in the darkness, the stars were turning. It was the last peace I would have for some time.

Erin died that night. Even now, all these years later, it is difficult to contemplate those words. In some ways it seems as incomprehensible now as it did when our bedside telephone rang and I first heard the terrible news.

The period that followed Erin's death was by far the darkest of my life. Jill and our friends were extraordinary in their love and support. Still, the loss was more than I could bear.

I wasn't going to kill myself with a pistol or with a rope. But I was, probably, going to kill myself with alcohol and drugs. Vodka and Valium was my cocktail of choice, and I was living recklessly and self-destructively.

My indifference to whether I lived or died was brought home to me once by the incredulous look of Dick Butera, a friend of mine, when we were on a Falcon-50, deadheading back to Aspen. Our pilot misread the altimeter and we came in much too fast, blowing every tire the second we hit the runway. For those few moments, I was convinced this was the end, but the plane skidded off the tarmac, into a huge snowdrift. When we finally came to a stop, Dick, who was sitting beside me in the back seat said, "Jesus, David." His expression was one of both shock and concern. When the tires went, he'd looked over at me and was puzzled to see that at that instant of extreme emergency I was smiling. It wasn't my life that flashed before my eyes. I had been picturing myself with Erin.

I believe I came very close to dying that day—and not only because of the calm acceptance that I felt when it seemed unlikely that I would survive. Jill was at our home in Aspen, preparing a light dinner for my arrival. At the very moment the plane had touched down, she looked up from the sink and was met with a startlingly clear vision of herself dressed in mourning. A short while later, I called from the airport to tell Jill not to worry. In case she'd heard anything on the radio about a plane crash at the airport, I wanted her to know that I was fine.

It was a strange, sad period. It felt like death was close

at hand.

There are a few pictures of me from that time. One is on a wall of framed photographs in Peter Munk's house in Toronto. I'm smiling at the camera the way people always do at social events, but Peter isn't taken in. "Look at the eyes," he says. "You can see the pain by looking at the eyes."

After that phone call, everything changed. At first, and for two years, it was a murky descent. It was as if someone who had always prided himself on his resolve, on his creativity, and on his youthful vigor had grown suddenly old. It was as if something that had always defined me—my simple joy in being alive—had been taken away. In short, I stopped caring. What were Hamlet's words? "How weary, stale, flat, and unprofitable seem to me all the uses of this world." It is not a period of my life I care to remember in great detail.

How appropriate, it seems to me now, that it was the winter solstice when the telephone rang. When the palm leaves were rattling in the night breeze and the little community of Lyford Cay was asleep in its own shadows. For it was as if, after I put down the receiver, a darkness had fallen around me that I could not escape. At first it was the darkness of anguish—of pain, of anger, of grief. It was the dark loneliness of loving someone to no avail. The pit in my stomach was like the sadness of incurable homesickness.

But somehow the days passed—first one, then the next, then the one after that. And somehow, after time, the awful words I heard on the phone that night became the darkness of my loss, my bitterness, my self-pity. I became the accumulative dark-ness of too many vodkas, too many pills, and too much hollow laughter. The shortest day, the longest night stretched on and on. That solstice became for me a winter in which it was all too easy to lose myself.

Jill tried desperately to help me through, and I doubt I would have survived without her love. But still, it was an awful period. How to break out of such a downward spiral? Nothing seemed capable of pulling me back. Finally, Jill organized a holiday that she hoped would free my mind from the painful circles in which it was spinning. And it was on that holiday that Erin saved me.

Erin was born in Toronto in 1961 and she had always had a wisdom far beyond her years. She was sweet and thoughtful, and her calm perspicacity was a great asset, particularly when it came to dealing with her father. My business interests were consuming in those days. I must have seemed, at times, more wayfarer than parent.

But Erin's love was a constant in my life. While growing up, she had stayed in Toronto with her mother, my first wife, Anna. Anna provided a stable home base, while my phone calls and postcards and letters came from the numerous ports of call of my business life. I came and went. I showed up here, we met there. I called to chat—from Hong Kong one week, Beirut the next. I was away so much it was sometimes not clear what I was "away" from.

A divorce is never uncomplicated, but Anna and I always tried to put Erin's well-being ahead of any differences we may have had. And so, with Anna's encouragement, Erin and I spent time together whenever we could—taking holidays in Aspen, or in London, or in Fiji. I remember those times with great fondness. Tousled blonde, green eyed, softly spoken, and deeply sensitive to those around her, she was a still point in my busy and restless life.

By the time Erin was 19, she was as much a friend as she was a daughter. I had married a second time, but sadly it proved to be short-lived. I enjoyed my bachelor days, but Erin could see that there was a loneliness at the core of my bonhomie. As a result, I took it very much to heart when one day she said: "Daddy, why don't you marry Jill? I've never seen you happier than you are when you're with her."

Not long after that, with Erin's advice ringing in my ears, I found myself doing what I should have done months, if not years earlier. I was on bended knee in Jill's flat in London, asking for her hand. My daughter's wise counsel proved to be the best I've ever been given.

A new marriage often requires some serious and sometimes difficult readjustment on the part of those who have been close to one member of a previous couple. Friends and family from an earlier life don't always accommodate themselves with ease to a new chapter. But I have to say that in our case things fell naturally into place. Unusually, for step-daughter and step-mother, Erin and Jill were the greatest of friends—real girl-friends, in fact. This could hardly have pleased me more. When Jill and I sailed from Southampton on the QE 2 on our honeymoon, Erin was on board.

The plans that were beginning to form for Jill and for me during our time in Lyford Cay would eventually crystallize with the construction of our home on Wakaya and The Wakaya Club and Spa.

Even though it had been land in Fiji that was the first investment of what would become Southern Pacific, Wakaya never quite fit into the company's plans. Peter Munk liked it well enough but was never drawn to it the way he is drawn to more rugged landscapes. He has a beautiful home in Switzerland and an island in northern Ontario. On a ski slope or watching the sunset in Georgian Bay is where he finds his peace.

I was a different story. From the moment I saw it, I couldn't get Wakaya out of my mind.

During our time in Lyford Cay, Jill and I began to imagine more than just a home on Wakaya. We began to dream of a community. We would build a home, of course, but we began to form the template for a resort that would be unlike any other on earth. A small, luxury resort on a rather big island. Terms such as "sustainability," "environmental footprint," and "organic" were far from being part of common parlance in those days, but I think, even then, we were feeling our way toward creating something that was not an artificial imposition, but that used the laws of nature and natural beauty as guiding principles. In our earliest planning, we may not have known what we wanted. We were, however, perfectly clear on what we didn't want, and that proved to be a useful starting point for our journey.

Our antipathy to the destructive force of mass tourism ensured that what we were picturing would impress the smallest possible footprint on the 2,200-acre island. We imagined a place that even at maximum capacity remained intimate. We dreamed of a place that would attract the most discerning, successful, interesting people—the kind of people we would truly welcome as our guests. We began talking of a place that would be so remarkable, and so restorative, it would have an impact on the lives of the people who found their way to it far beyond that of a more ordinary travel destination.

The resort would require trained, dedicated staff, which meant the island would also have a village, a school, a church, and other amenities for our employees. These are all aspects of Wakaya that are now reality, and The Wakaya Club and Spa now has a reputation—as reported in *Town & Country, Travel + Leisure,* and *The Hideaway Report,* among other international magazines—as one of the most special resorts in the world. This is what we really wanted to do. An undertaking that was fuelled by our passion for excellence and our desire to create a unique community and preserve a place of great beauty, far more than it was fuelled by commercial considerations.

Our ideas—slowly gathering clarity as we talked and

dreamed together during our time in Lyford Cay—grew organically from our love of Wakaya. I'd felt a spiritual bond with the island ever since I first set foot on it in 1972. Erin had always loved it. To my delight, Jill had fallen under its spell on her first visit in 1976.

There is a Beatles song—"In My Life"—that touches on one of the reasons Jill and I hold Wakaya so dear: "There are places I remember / All my life, though some have changed / Some forever, not for better / Some have gone, and some remain." As much as the lyrics, the song's wistful melody catches the sadness of paradises lost. These kinds of disappearances are a staple of our lives and of history. After all, change is the only constant in this world. Still, I sometimes think that in my life, the changes have been particularly sudden and particularly dramatic. Here one day. Gone the next. Much like youth.

Cannes, St. Tropez, Marbella, Acapulco, Puerto Vallarta, Hawaii—these are a few of the places that, as the song goes, I'll remember all my life. I happened to be young at a time when they were at their best. In the 1950s, when I first visited Majorca, for example, there were all of four hotels on the island. The one that fell sufficiently within my range of affordability and basic comfort was a little place on the bay of Camp de Mar. It had twelve rooms, a ten-seat restaurant, and a small beachside cottage that just happened to be available to me—for $11 a week.

Such perfectly simple beauty branded itself on me. It's never been something I've been willing to give up trying to find.

I so easily see myself, in days gone by, swimming out to

a yacht that I discovered moored one morning when I woke in my little beach house in Majorca. I was curious about who had dropped anchor overnight and merely being sociable. Imagine my surprise when the skipper turned out to be Errol Flynn. He invited me aboard for drinks a little earlier in the day than was my custom. He was quite as charming as any fan of his movies would expect him to be. We became friends—oh, so long ago.

I can picture myself, sitting at a sidewalk café in Cannes, swimming in the crystal waters of Acapulco, strolling through the narrow streets of Puerto Vallarta. But all these places are now not what they once were. Few places are.

Most people I know take these kinds of changes—the bigger hotels, the crowded beaches, the frenetic pace of rampant commercialism—as the inevitable price of progress. The way of the world, they say. Nothing to be done. But for some reason, I can never shrug off these transformations.

They have always left me with a profound sense of loss—an emptiness, an absence, a grieving apprehension of things disappearing. Everyone experiences these kinds of sadnesses: I wish my father had lived to see my business successes. I wish that I had a recording of my mother's beautiful singing. One by one, loved ones and old friends disappear. I have to remind myself, for example, that David Niven is no longer with us, so vivid is my sense of his delightful presence in my life. Jill so loved listening to David's wonderful stories, and she was such an appreciative audience, that he came to call her "the girl with the dark brown laughter." What a sad day it was for us when, in the early 1980s, we learned that he would not be able to come visit us on

Wakaya. One of his two sons, Jamie, has written movingly about that period:

"He called me one day in late 1980 and was worried that he had not sounded right in a television interview with Michael Parkinson that had been taped several nights before. I had a look at the show and I thought he looked rather thin and might have suffered a small stroke. We chatted about that and he decided to take himself out to the Mayo Clinic in Rochester, Minnesota, and let the doctors there try and figure it out. He spent several days there undergoing a variety of tests and finally called me and said, "Well I did not have a stroke but I have something called Lou Gehrig's disease and it is going to kill me."

He was actually planning a trip to visit us at Wakaya when his illness finally became too much for him to manage. He died in 1983. And because we felt he should be remembered for his spirit of youthful fun, we constructed a memorial to him at The Wakaya Club. I like to think it is exactly what he would have wished. The plaque reads: "The David Niven Croquet Court."

Some might say that's just how things go. But I am not entirely reconciled to these kinds of changes.

I feel a deep need to hold onto something that cannot be taken away. Jill shares this vision. As a result, we have decided to work together to create a place that will never be spoiled.

A favourite quote of mine is used as a preface to one of The Wakaya Club and Spa's brochures, and it pretty much sums up why we have fallen so deeply in love with Wakaya, and why we are so intent on preserving it. "The more the world changes, the more we gravitate to places that don't."

There is nothing more shattering than a bedside telephone ringing suddenly in the darkness. It never sounds like good news.

I don't think I was yet awake that night in Lyford Cay as I fumbled for the receiver. It was two o'clock in the morning. Jill stirred from her sleep beside me. My voice was thick with slumber. Jill heard me say, "Hello?"

It was Erin's mother, calling from Toronto. Anna was saying something to me. It made no sense.

There was a pause. And then Jill heard me say, "Pardon?" There was another pause.

When I spoke again there was something in my voice—a suddenly alert, measured need to take in information—that awakened Jill completely. In the dark, she heard me say: "Would you repeat that, please?"

Wakaya is a place that Erin had always loved.

Over the years, we'd had many of our happiest father-daughter holidays together there. Amid so much interruption, travel, and change, I'd come to see Wakaya as a solid foundation in our lives. Anna's home was Erin's home, of course. But Wakaya was our place. Erin and I returned to it again and again. In some ways, I'd watched her grow up there.

I had always loved the pleasure she took in exploring the island. Her love of nature blossomed on the beaches, the coral reefs, and along the forest paths of Wakaya. How thrilled she would be by the organic agricultural programs we are so intent to bring to full fruition now.

It was as if Erin sensed that Wakaya was, in some way, the very essence of the natural world. And it's true. On Wakaya, as you watch the slowly lengthening sunsets, as you sit and listen to the waves roll in from the Koro Sea, as you gaze up at the Southern Cross and the infinite clarity of a star-spread night, you can feel that what you are seeing is a beauty that is so ancient it makes the histories of Captain Bligh, or the whalers, or the old tribal wars seem almost recent. Sometimes, in Fiji, one has the sense of looking back through the millennia to an undiscovered paradise. Its beauty is so unblemished it feels as if it comes directly from the beginning of time. Sometimes, it feels to me as if Wakaya could be Eden.

My interest in preschools is part of Erin's legacy. She loved young children. In Fiji, there was always a gang of little kids trailing in her wake. I've chosen not to be haunted by the fact that the summer before her death she asked me if she could stay in Fiji for the year and teach, and I said I thought she should return to Toronto and complete her education, a decision that had unforeseeable results.

Rather than engaging in the futile chase of "if only," I've taken the wish Erin expressed as a sign that has pointed me in an extraordinarily satisfying direction. The more involved in the development of preschools I become—in Fiji, in San Diego, in Las Vegas, and in Florida—the more I am convinced of their value. As of today, my charitable Trust has built nine pre-schools, and contributed to countless more by the provision of professional development materials to pre-school teachers.

Studies have shown that to an astonishing extent, a personality is formed between the ages of three and nine. And so the lessons learned in preschool—respect for others, dignity of self, responsibility, learning the difference between right and wrong, and, perhaps most important, learning how to learn—not only give a child a huge advantage, they can overcome what might otherwise have proven to be crippling disadvantages. Andre Agassi speaks even more passionately on the subject than I do because he has seen the results when the children leave preschool and enter his charter school. He says that it's a different student altogether—and that, in many cases, the whole social milieu around the child has been dramatically improved. The values that are taught in our preschools have a positive influence on the student's family—siblings and other relatives. It's like a widening circle created by the pebble we drop in the underprivileged pond. It has had a stunning effect. Erin would be proud of this. Of that, I have no doubt.

Our life in Lyford Cay had a pace that suited us. But Jill and I understood that it was not to be a permanent stay.

We were at a crossroads in our lives. And among the many decisions facing us was where we would make our home base. I was trying to decide whether, like Peter Munk, I wanted to make Canada my place of residence. In many ways, returning to Toronto would have been the natural choice. I'd been born in Winnipeg and raised in Toronto, and I had always had a strong attachment to the country where I'd grown up.

Being a Canadian, even expat one, is not always easy. It's remarkable what assumptions can be made about a place that is, to the world, so often obscured by America's bright lights. Even history is sometimes lost in the glare. For example, I often have to explain to my American friends that while the contribution of the United States to the First and Second World Wars cannot be exaggerated, they were not entirely unassisted in their efforts. Canada entered the First World War in 1914, two years and many, many casualties before the United States. Canada entered the Second World War in 1939, 18 months before Pearl Harbor. In the First World War, Canada lost 65,000 of her sons in some of the most vicious battles the world had ever seen.

In 1983, by the night of that dreadful winter solstice, Canada was very much on my mind.

Earlier that month, I had travelled to Toronto to see Erin and to attend her mother's annual Christmas party. I had been thinking of asking Erin to join Jill and me in the Bahamas over the Christmas holidays. It was always such a pleasure to spend time with her, and I knew that it was sometimes a great relief for her to escape a week or two of Canadian winter.

In Toronto, I could see that Erin was happy. Her mother was still living in what had been our home when we were married—the same house, in fact, that had been my parents' on Oriole Parkway. I was pleased that Anna and Erin were there, but it was always, under the circumstances of a divorce, a little strange for me to return to the house where I had grown up. But one takes these things in stride. And Anna was a gracious hostess. Her Christmas party was always a very happy occasion.

The house was full of friends and family. There were many familiar faces. But as I stood there, surrounded by so many people, I could see that I was a distraction for Erin. She had friends and school chums at her home that night, and her instinct to keep me company and to make sure I was enjoying myself was getting in the way of her enjoyment of them. And so, eventually, I just slipped away. I was returning to the Bahamas the next day. I decided not to confuse matters by suggesting to Erin that she return with me to Nassau.

On my flight back, I found myself thinking about my immediate future. Toronto can have a wonderfully festive quality at Christmas. Were I to move back, I'd be closer to Erin. It would be easy to slip back in to a way of life with which I was quite familiar. As my flight left the Canadian winter behind, I was trying to imagine what it would be like to live there again.

By 1983, Toronto was a far more interesting place than the

dull, rather stodgy city in which I had grown up. Still, I wasn't at all sure about returning. I was a confirmed internationalist. My professional life had embraced globalization long before the term became part of everyday speech. In the previous 12 years I'd lived in London and New York, with short periods in Sydney, Egypt, and Fiji. I was now giving serious thought to living primarily in the United States. New York City was a place that I loved. Even then—even as it was emerging from a dark period of urban decay—it seemed one of the most exciting cities on earth.

Jill and I had come to Nassau to allow ourselves time to settle into the right long-term decision. And time was what we needed. We needed to slow things down for a bit, and give our future some careful thought. The only two things we knew for certain were that we would be together and that, wherever we made our home base, there was one place on earth that would be an important part of our lives. Wakaya was, even by then, a treasure to which Jill and I were intent on holding.

When, during our last holiday in Fiji, Erin asked me if she could take the year off and teach at the school on the island, I could see that it was a tempting idea for her. She was very serious about the request, and it was clear to me that Erin would make an excellent teacher. She had an extraordinary gift for communicating with young people. But I felt there would be lots of opportunities to take a year off. I advised her to return to Toronto to complete her education. I thought there would be plenty of time.

"What is it?" Jill asked. Even in the darkness of our bedroom in Lyford Cay, she could tell that something was very wrong.

I held the receiver and turned to her. "Erin," I said. Even as I repeated what Anna had told me, it seemed impossible.

"Erin was killed in her apartment. In Toronto. Earlier tonight." I found it difficult to pronounce the word. "Murdered."

Somehow I got up. It was as if I were trapped in a nightmare, and I suppose I felt that if I made my way through the shadows I could find my way out of it. I must have found my way from the bedroom. From what seemed like far away, I could hear Jill crying.

I passed through the darkness of our house to the living room. Some light was coming through the front windows. I looked out. It seemed impossible that Lyford Cay could remain so tranquil.

I must have been naked because I remember that when I collapsed there was nothing between my skin and the hard cold floor. I have no idea how long I was there. It was dark for a long time, but it wasn't the kind of darkness that disappeared with the dawn.

We were in a strange little hotel in the south of France. We were on the holiday that Jill had organized to help me try to get my mind off Erin's death, and I woke up in the middle of the night to find Erin sitting at the foot of my bed.

I can't honestly say whether it was a dream, or a vision, or a visitation. I suppose they amount to the same thing. But whatever one chooses to call it, her presence was vivid. She felt absolutely real to me. And she asked me the most extraordinary question.

My daughter said: "Daddy, do you love me?"

I was stunned. "Darling, of course I do," I replied.

"Then why are you living this way? If you loved me you wouldn't be doing this to yourself."

And that was that. I fell back to sleep. The next morning, when I woke up, the first thing I did was flush my Valium down the toilet. I began to live again. There was so much to live for.

That Erin's murder remained unsolved felt strangely irrelevant to me. It still does. She was stalked. She was attacked. Her killer slipped away into the Toronto night.

All death, I suppose, is a kind of mystery to the living. Solved or unsolved, Erin's death was totally bewildering. It will always remain so.

I remember that not long after her death, a Toronto homicide detective called to tell me that they were sure they had a lead. He seemed excited. He was trying to do his job, and I tried to appear interested in the direction of his investigation. Erin, the detective informed me, had been seen a few weeks earlier walking hand-in-hand with an older man. They had been seen together, crossing a busy street—in Aspen. And as the detective spoke my heart sank at the futility of it all. The older man had been me. Erin and I had been together in Aspen only a few weeks before.

The killer's identity meant nothing. It had nothing to do with what little was left and with all that had disappeared.

The sorrow has never entirely receded, of course. The loss has never lessened. But gradually, over more time, with Jill's love, and with the love and support of friends and family, I was able to find a way to correct my course, and to turn my sadness from something that was eating away at me into something positive, into a force on which I could thrive. I was able to become someone, once again, of whom my only child would be proud. "Do you love me, Daddy?" Erin asked on that memorable night in the strange little hotel in the south of France. And the question made me realize that her legacy was something I could create. Indeed, it was something I had to create.

Erin's legacy is my devotion to the cause of preschool education. It's the pleasure I take in my work and in my friends. It's my love for Jill. It's our creation of something truly beautiful on the island in Wakaya. It's the pride I take when I stand overlooking the lush interior valleys of Wakaya and inspect our paddocks of thriving organic ginger. It's something lasting, something protected, something cherished in a world where all too often the beautiful is destroyed or allowed to disappear. It's the delight I take, sitting here now, on the deck of Sega na Leqa, our island home, with my papers, and my notes, and my old photographs, and with these memories spread out before me.

Here the only sound is the wind, and the gentle splashing of water from fountains, and the calls of the birds that inhabit the canopy of trees. I am looking out over the turquoise of the Koro Sea. Years ago, I realized that it was in my power to turn a legacy from the darkness into which I was sinking and make it something bright and beautiful and full of delight—just like the tousled blonde little girl whose face appears among the other children in the stained-glass window behind the altar of Wakaya's pretty little church.

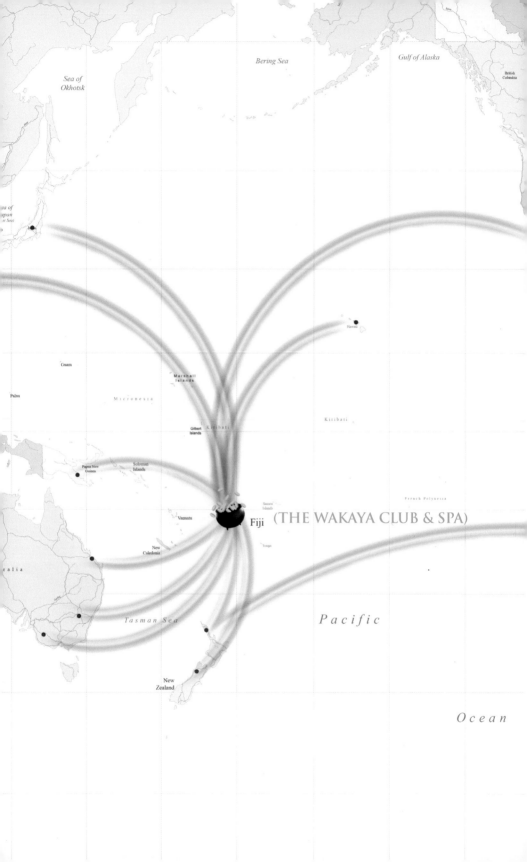

ALL THAT GLISTENS

"A pessimist sees the difficulty in every opportunity; an optimist sees the opportunity in every difficulty."
—Sir Winston Churchill

IT TOOK TWO THINGS TO START SOUTHERN PACIFIC HOTELS—
an investment and an idea. The idea was simple; the best ones
often are. We believed that by rationalizing the hotels and resorts
we acquired—by streamlining management, by capitalizing on
the economies of scale our holdings created, by coordinating
personnel and pooling talent and expertise—we could run each
hotel more efficiently and more effectively than had been previously possible. This has always been a rule of mine: Invest in
people. However impressive your office tower, however wonderful your company art collection, your best investment will always
be in the people you employ. Their experience, their expertise,
but mostly their energy and dedication—these are invariably a
company's greatest assets.

We started Southern Pacific with a $300,000 investment,
and it steadily grew. In 1974, we bought the Trust Houses Forte
Group's minority interest in Southern Pacific—a transaction that,
as the business writer Garth Hopkins put it, "consolidated our
position as the major hotel operator in the South Pacific." Even-

tually, we sold the company for $128 million.

That is an entirely satisfactory return on investment. No one could think otherwise. Peter and I were both pleased. Who wouldn't be? But the really important thing about Southern Pacific's success is this: The difference between our original investment and the selling price represents wealth far beyond what Peter and I made personally. The profits of our successful idea spread a wide circle, from our most junior employee to the banks and the brokerage houses that were our financial associates.

The story is similar with Barrick Gold. Peter and I started that company with a $40 million investment. Our first acquisition, in 1984, was a smallish mine in northern Ontario, near the town of Wawa, but that same year we took a major forward step when we purchased control of Camflo Mining—after assuring a skittish Royal Bank of Canada that Camflo's $100 million debt would be repaid within a year (it was). I was sent twice into the lion's den during the process of our acquisition. Once to talk with our new employees in northern Quebec. I addressed the Camflo miners at a town-hall style meeting to assure them that the new owners wanted to build on the team we had inherited, that our intention was to take the company to the next level. I'd been nervous about this session, but I tried not to show it when I stood to speak, and once I began speaking frankly about our ambitions, the meeting went well.

My other job was much less pleasant. I was called upon to be polite and gently cajoling during two lunches with Camflo's chairman and controlling shareholder. He was being a bit sticky on the deal. I needed to figure out why, and to find a way around his obstructionism.

Obviously, we needed to secure his cooperation, and I had imagined that he had a complex business rationale for his reluctance to relinquish control. I'd tried to guess in advance what the obstacles might be, and I had prepared my counter-proposals to his objections. As is often the case with the unknown, his reluctance was based on something much less complicated than I had imagined.

It didn't take me long to realize that his reason was much simpler and much darker than I could have guessed. His stated "I'll never do business with Peter Munk" was, so it gradually became clear, a euphemism for "I'll never do business with that Jew." Aha, I thought, so that's it. I remember sitting across from him, smiling and chatting amiably, nudging him closer and closer toward agreement with Barrick, and feeling the grim satisfaction that spies and undercover agents must sometimes feel when mingling successfully with the enemy.

In the early days at Barrick, we approached gold mines exactly as we had approached hotels at Southern Pacific. Streamlining management, pooling talent and expertise, allows the smallest mining operation to take advantage of the company as a whole. Our overall strategy was clear: to utilize the forward gold market to achieve higher prices while providing downside protection in weak gold markets. Barrick took advantage of spikes in the gold market to deliver against spot-deferred contracts. We earned interest on gold reserves still in the ground.

The strategy worked. And once again, a wide sphere has

profited from our investment and from the company's animating strategy and philosophy. Our $40 million investment is now worth $38 billion, and the truth is that Barrick's broad network has made far more money than either Peter or I have. Which is as it should be. That is why capitalism works.

☥

Winston Churchill was fond of quoting the French historian François Guizot's famous aphorism: "Any man who is not a socialist at 20 has no heart; and any man who is not a conservative at 40 has no head." There is great wisdom in those words. Certainly, they ring true for me, except that the time frame of my own conversion from left to right was a little tighter than the 20 years described by Monsieur Guizot.

In 1951, my European travels were coming to an end. A reluctant end, I have to say. But as much as I was enjoying my continental sojourn, there was no getting around the fact that I was very close to running out of money. I've known people who have never learned this basic lesson of economics: Don't live beyond your means. In fact, I've known millionaires who have lived like billionaires, and their stories often conclude as unhappily as those of prodigals of much more modest means. In my case, the "bald tire" ruse had not worked. My father read me like a book. It was time to come home.

I found a berth on a student ship. It was a converted troop ship sailing from Le Havre. Most of the passengers were young idealists who had been studying at the Sorbonne. The idea was that their studies would actually continue on board, and so every day of the passage, lectures were given by professors of history and economics and political science—most of whom, as it happened, were committed leftists.

At the time I was, I suppose, a socialist of sorts. I was concerned about poverty. I was angered by inequity. I was worried about injustice. It was impossible not to be. I'd seen the utter devastation of the war and the misery it had left in its wake. And these concerns had pushed my political point of view toward the kinds of solutions espoused in those days by left-wing politicians, writers, and pundits. This wasn't at all an unusual position for a young person to take—even a young person who came from a background that was as solidly pro–free enterprise as mine.

There was no mistaking where Dad's political convictions lay. He was a dyed-in-the-wool capitalist, managing director of one of Canada's leading investment houses, and someone who, even when disguised in dungarees, work boots, and an old pullover, could never pass as a man of the people.

When I was a teenager, during one of the holidays that our family spent at the working farm we called Far Hills, I accompanied my father to the bank in the nearby town of Aurora.

Dad had been doing some work on our property that day, and he was dressed in his well-worn farming clothes. He needed to write a few cheques and make a withdrawal, and as he was doing so the bank's new manager began to chat with him in a friendly, casual way.

The manager asked my father what he thought of the prospects of a particular stock—I think it was Falconbridge. I could see that my father was a little surprised by the question. Customarily, a bank manager would not solicit financial advice from a client. But my father began to reply, in his customarily well-informed way, about his views on the company's performance. But after a few sentences, the manager interrupted him.

"Thank you, Mr. Gilmour," he said. "Sorry to have troubled you. I just needed to make sure that you really were Harrison Gilmour."

I could hardly have come from a more pro-business background, but that did not mean narrow-minded. My father had supported me in my decision to travel because he thought it was important for me to see the world and to think about it for myself. And thinking about the world in those days inevitably meant considering alternative political points of view. Europe was rebuilding itself after the calamity of the Second World War, and leftist voices were prominent in the debates that surrounded reconstruction. It had been less than a decade since the Soviet Union had been our allies in the struggle against fascism (there were more than 25 million war dead in the Soviet Union alone), and the almost incomprehensible crimes of Stalin were still largely unknown in the West. The cries of alarm from dissidents in Estonia, Poland, Lithuania, and Georgia were viewed by many as merely the inevitable creaks and groans of a new world order. Few people in the West had even heard the name Alexander Solzhenitsyn.

The Hungarian revolution was still in the future; the brief

Czech spring further in the future still. The Berlin Wall would not go up until 1961. Indeed, the term "Iron Curtain" was still relatively new. Winston Churchill, who had not lost the ability to see things for what they were, coined the expression in 1946 in a speech at Westminster College in Fulton, Missouri, where he was accepting an honourary degree.

America, of course, had never embraced socialism as a real political alternative: Senator Joe McCarthy was still a force to be reckoned with. But elsewhere in the world, left-wing policies were finding their way into the mainstream. To be a socialist, or a leftist, or even a member of the Communist Party was no more extreme a political position than, for example, supporting Greenpeace would be today. Or possibly the Canadian Liberal Party.

The world was looking for a new way—and the search was often more passionate than judicious. Despite his wartime heroics, Churchill had been defeated by Clement Attlee's Labour Party in the election of 1945. Attlee was famously described by Churchill as a modest man who had a good deal to be modest about. It was an apt description, but the British people were looking for a new direction. This slap in the face to the man who had saved England in its darkest hour was a political reversal that, to this day, I confess, I find incomprehensible. It infuriates me still. But it was part of a postwar trend toward the left—which may have something to do with how passionately I hold to my political convictions today.

In my eight million miles of travel, I have never found a place where socialism actually worked. And when I witnessed, at first hand, the rubble, the pain, and the devastation that was the aftermath in Europe of the Second World War, I began to wonder where the wealth would come from that was required for rebuilding. Inspired leadership was necessary, of course. But so was the injection of capital and creative energy that only capitalism could provide. Unfortunately, this was a perspective that was far from fashionable at the time.

In Britain, and, later, in Canada, state-supported healthcare systems were in the process of being created (I have too often personally witnessed the unfortunate and disastrous toll taken by the often cited Canadian socialist healthcare system on many friends and colleagues.) In Italy and in France, communist parties were legitimate and influential. And in Paris, a city that cheered the GIs who had helped liberate it, the little Volkswagen I'd bought kept getting its convertible roof slashed because of the foreign license plates. A foreigner with enough money to own a car in Paris, even as proletarian a vehicle as the most humble Volkswagen, was, so it appeared to some so-called activists, obviously a car owned by an American. As the old saying goes, no good turn shall go unpunished.

My slashed roof notwithstanding, it wasn't difficult for a young man to be sympathetic to the leftist point of view in those days. Socialism was fashionable for one thing, and, regrettably, one should never underestimate the power of trendiness in political discourse, especially when it involves the young. It was quite à la mode to be quoting Marx and Sartre in Parisian cafés in the early 1950s. Naïvety has never got in the way of youthful political fads, as so many supporters of Pelosi, or Royal, or Zapatero make all too clear today.

Many of the economic and social inequities that the leftists took such delight in pointing out were very real. I had seen that for myself. The chief purpose of travel—and the reason why it should be so important an aspect of anyone's education—is that you see what the world is really like. In a column that appeared in the *International Herald Tribune* on March 13, 2007, Nicholas D. Kristof wondered what the root causes might be of some of America's recent foreign policy blunders, and he concluded that "Part of the problem is that American universities do an execrable job preparing students for global citizenship.... That is one reason why I always exhort college students to take a 'gap year' and roam the world...."

It may have been that because I was returning home my thoughts were beginning to turn to my future. I was not at all clear on what I would do, but I must have been aware of an emerging sense of who I was. I must have been beginning to dream about what I wanted to do with my life. I would not yet have been able to use a term as specific as "entrepreneur," but I was beginning to realize that the excitement with which I contemplated the future was based, in large part, on the prospect of putting to use an energy and imagination that defined me as an individual.

On board ship, I sat in on many of the lectures—to begin with. But they had a curious effect. They made me realize that the world those leftist professors was conjuring for their impressionable students was a world in which I would not be able to function. It became more and more clear to me that the future they hoped for was not one I could believe in. They were very good at describing a socialist utopia; the only problem was, it didn't seem to have a place for anyone like me. In a system based entirely on redistribution of wealth, I couldn't see any place for wealth to be created in the first place.

Contrary to the expectations of the student ship's organizers, I began to see a conjunction between my prospects and the great good fortune of having been born into a political and economic system that would allow me to fulfill them. I realized, rather to my surprise, that my hope lay in a different direction than most of my (you'll excuse the expression) fellow travellers. I realized I had no interest in becoming part of a movement. Suddenly, with a new clarity, I could see the truth of Winston Churchill's famously double-edged observation: "The inherent vice of capitalism is the unequal sharing of blessings; the inherent virtue of socialism is the unequal sharing of miseries."

I stood at the rail of that ship, looking out over the steel-grey water of the North Atlantic. I was looking forward to becoming who I wanted to be, and I was only too pleased to be returning to a system and to an economy that would allow me to do so.

In many professions, the older one gets, the easier the path. This is not necessarily true for the entrepreneur.

A start-up is a start-up is a start-up. Each is unique, and each has its own challenges. There are lessons to be learned, certainly, but there are as many exceptions as there are rules. It's always a new journey—and there is never much of a map. This can be unnerving at times. But the upside is that things rarely, if ever, get dull. In fact, I sometimes wonder if I haven't lived the life I have principally because I have such a low tolerance for monotony. Whatever else can be said about the unknown, exploring it is rarely boring.

This urge to reach for something in the unknown is not shared by everyone. Some people don't care for the dark. Some don't like uncertainty. Some of the most successful business people I know are brilliant salespeople, so long as they are selling what is already right in front of them. Others are excellent managers, so long as they are managing what is already established and clearly defined. Not everyone copes well with the risk that comes, hand in hand, with invention.

You can either be excited by not knowing what lies ahead, or frightened by it. I think I'm naturally more inclined to the former. Even as a boy, I was genuinely puzzled by friends who, from the age of 14 or so, had simply accepted the wishes of their parents when it came to their choice of career. That didn't seem wise to me, even then. Nor did it seem much fun.

There is something about entrepreneurialism that depends on a kind of faith—a belief that uncertainty is not a terrifying barrier, but a necessary part of the process, as full of possibility as it is fraught with risk. It's something you're born with, I think. You have to believe that things happen for a reason, that there are always lessons to be learned from setbacks and disappointments, but that ultimately there is a goal toward which you are moving. You have to be able to trust yourself.

I have always felt that my experiences have been leading me somewhere. In my youth, my travels taught me lessons before I understood the need to learn them. The demise of Clairtone was a huge disappointment, but one that taught me which business practices to embrace and which to avoid. Even something as shattering, as catastrophic, and as tragic as Erin's death has, over time, taken on a meaning that I could never have imagined when I was tumbling into my dark hole of anger, pain, and self pity in her murder's aftermath.

The pain was intolerable. The loss of so beautiful a child, the violence of her death, and the fact that whoever the madman was who had followed her to her Toronto apartment on that terrible December night and killed her still remained at large, was more than I could bear.

Not a day goes by, even still, when I don't find myself wishing that we could all somehow go back in time and side-step Erin's fate. How I wish she were here to see what we have achieved. And yet, after the dark period that followed her death, it's as if Erin somehow reclaimed for me the goodness of her legacy. Gradually, the negativity of anger and the bitterness were replaced with the kind of positive endeavours now linked in my mind with Erin—principally our commitment to Wakaya and our philanthropic focus on preschool education. But the shakeup that I went through—my downward spiral and the eventual correction of that sad, lonely spin—seemed also to inspire me to take stock of my professional life. I came to realize that my role with TrizecHahn and with Barrick had blurred into one that had more to do with financial strategies, the management of assets, and corporate governance than with creative capitalism. I concluded that I needed to reorder things so that I could focus on doing what I do best: start things up. And once I did, this decision felt immediately right. It was as if I was able to remember something of the excitement and anticipation I felt when I stood at the rail of that converted troop ship, outbound from Le Havre. I was able to remember who I wanted to be.

Entrepreneurs are not born, they are born of life's experiences. It has been my ongoing need to reach for something that is not yet there, to peer into the future and wonder "what if" that makes me believe I have become an entrepreneur to the core. And when an instinct is this deeply rooted, it needs to find fulfillment. If it doesn't, unhappiness is the inevitable result. The frustrations can be seen as not merely obstacles, but as signs that somehow the wrong road has been chosen. There are people in all walks of life, rich and poor, who have never got off the wrong road—and there are not many people for whom I feel more sorry. I've been fortunate in that eventually, I found my way.

In the late 1990s, I found myself at odds with my fellow directors on the board of Barrick Gold. This was not simply a disagreement. This was a case of my voice no longer being heard.

Under discussion was Barrick's proposed expansion into China, an idea that many of my fellow board members looked on with unbridled enthusiasm. Then, as now, China beckoned. Then, as now, I had grave misgivings. I could see the possibility of an enormous expense of the executive's and the board's time, the company's resources and creative energies, on a venture that was doomed from the outset.

As national economies go, China's is singularly self-centred. Foreign companies are welcomed with banquets and speeches and then, once knowledge and investment have been leveraged by their obliging hosts, the companies are waved goodbye—usually within five years' time.

American Motors and Foster's Brewery learned this truth the hard way. I thought that Barrick would do well to avoid similar disappointment. I said so, and my view had some evidence to support it. I felt the Chinese were unlikely to relinquish ownership of a commodity so closely linked to national security as gold. As well, I knew that gold deposits were owned by the provinces and not by the central government, and (as all Canadians know) the provinces of a country are seldom in harmony with a federal government. In China in those days, gold was regulated and protected by myriad levels of government—all functioning with agendas that, to an outsider, were far from transparent.

A cousin of mine was the Canadian trade commissioner to China. Because of his fluency in Chinese he often overheard more than his hosts thought he did. He confirmed for me the legitimacy of my concerns. I became convinced that no matter what we did, no matter how effusively we were welcomed by our Chinese hosts and how splendidly we were wined and dined, we were not going to meet with success.

Our board at Barrick was composed of luminaries such as former Canadian Prime Minister Brian Mulroney and the noted businessman Paul Desmarais. It was chaired by Peter Munk, and it could hardly have been better connected with the highest levels of the Chinese government. But I was strongly opposed to the company's proposed move into China, and I said so. For my troubles, I was told I was "out of touch."

Concerns are pointless if they have no expression in the practical world. And living with worry, as opposed to acting on concern, is not a helpful role for a member of a board to play. A life is too short to waste in activity that has no effect on others— and a board member's chief responsibility is to inform and, if necessary, influence the opinions of the board as a whole. I felt that my situation was thrown into even higher relief by virtue of the fact that the Barrick board was made up of people for whom I have nothing but respect and admiration. That my voice was not contributing to consensus awoke me to the realization that I was in limbo, biding my time for whatever new challenge would point the way to my future.

I suppose I could have thrown some kind of hissy fit. I suppose I could have demanded a more cogent response to my concerns. But I could see that minds were set, and nothing I could say would change them. In such a situation, the only good option is to make a graceful exit.

After considerable soul-searching, I resigned as a director. Even though my isolated point of view was eventually proven to be prescient—Barrick's China venture was fruitless—resigning from the board of a company I had helped to found was not a happy event in my life.

However, an entrepreneur learns that a painful "no" can actually be pointing to a much bigger "yes"—if you are willing to keep your eyes open for opportunity. Realizing what you don't want to do is often the first step to understanding what you do. Both involve following instincts. If you have to design buildings, you're an architect. If you have to act, you're an actor. If you have to start businesses, you're an entrepreneur. In other words, the work has to be what you most want, not the results of the work. As I have often said, money is not the goal. But money is an excellent measure of how good your work is.

Had I not resigned from Barrick, my life would have taken a very different course. I would not have been able to focus so completely on FIJI Water—and no business venture is successful without focus, focus, and more focus. Had it not been so successful, FIJI Water might not have led me to more recent ventures such as *VIV*, Zinio and Wakaya Perfection.

As well, this experience confirmed for me something that I'd long suspected, but that I now recognize as a truth solid enough to live by: There are people who are very good at being on boards, and there are people who are not. I have received many kind offers of directorships, and while I am invariably flattered to be asked, I always turn them down. My talents lie elsewhere.

Success of one form or another does not mean that

someone will necessarily have the organizational skills that make for a good board member. Indeed, in my experience, there are always people on boards who, really, should never be there at all—a proposition that I doubt will be very strenuously disputed by anyone who has spent much time sitting on boards. Over 50 years of board duty have made me something of an expert in spotting the varieties of the species.

Everyone who has ever been on a board knows the types I am describing. The board member who reads the minutes on the flight to the meeting, and who comes up with one cogent remark in order to demonstrate that they have taken their duties seriously. Or the ones who don't quite manage to stay awake, and who sneak a little nap during the presentation by the chair of the finance committee. Or the ones who doodle, or check their smartphones, or who—most brazenly—attend to the business of other businesses during the presentation of a lengthy report.

Some people join boards because they feel a responsibility to take part in the process of governance, even though matters of governance are not their strong suit. Theirs is a laudable if misguided contribution to a company's or an institution's well-being. Others operate at a much more shallow level. They enjoy the travel, and the parties, and the dinners that come with board membership. They embrace what I call the four "P's"—perks, privilege, power, and prestige—of the directors' boardroom. And it is a minority—sometimes I think, a small minority—who sit on boards because they are very good at the job.

It's a question of knowing yourself, of recognizing that we all have different talents, priorities, and areas of expertise, and that some of us—and I include myself in this category—are more creative in nature than bureaucratic, more inclined to build than to organize, more naturally disposed to invention than management. It's not that an entrepreneur has better things to do. Boards of directors have an important role and a great responsibility. Had certain boards been more cognizant of their responsibilities, instead of providing a rubber stamp for a forceful CEO, we might not have witnessed some of the corporate disgraces of recent years. But entrepreneurs, in my experience, can frequently balance the equation of time spent and reward more effectively outside the boardroom. Their brains tend to work better "off agenda." They tend to find their ideas outside the box.

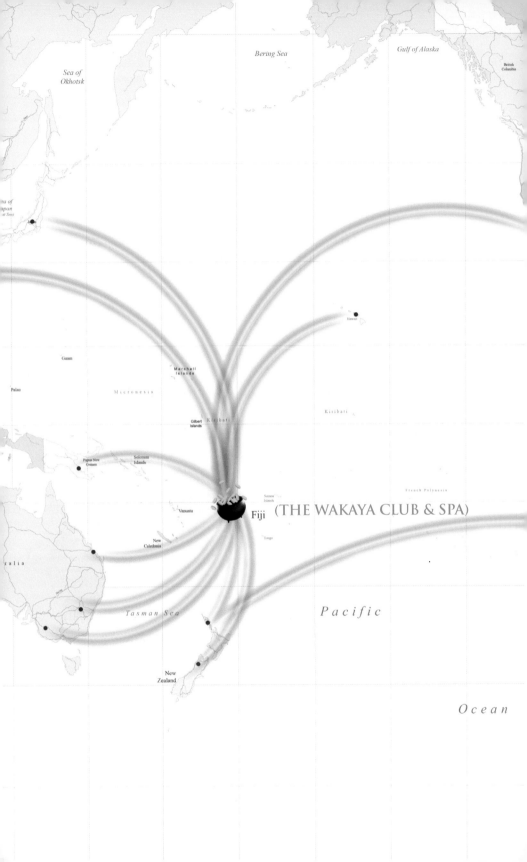

THE SOURCE

"Some people regard free enterprise as a predatory tiger to be shot. Others look on it as a cow they can milk. Not enough people see it as a healthy horse pulling a sturdy wagon."
—Sir Winston Churchill

IN THEIR REMARKABLE BOOK, WATER AND SALT, Barbara Hendel and Peter Ferreira write of the unique origins and qualities of Fiji's natural artesian water. Hendel is a medical doctor who has been working as a holistic health practitioner for over 20 years. Ferreira is a biophysicist, and their combined perspective was a revelation to me. The passage I have in mind is worth quoting at some length since, as the subtitle of their book makes clear, the subject is of considerable importance. In fact, everything depends on it. Water is indeed "the essence of life."

"At the centre of the macroscopic universe, in solitary isolation, surrounded for thousands of miles by the Pacific Ocean, lies one of the world's last strongholds of ecological sanctity, the Fiji islands. The more than 330 islands are ecological jewels, whereas the mainland of Viti Levu, with its volcanic highlands and tropical rainforests, represents a one-of-a-kind natural ecosystem. Safe from pollution, pesticides, and acid rain, the islands are located some 1,500 miles from the nearest continent and have no polluting industry of their own; one might call these remote Fiji islands paradise.

"The secret to our precious resources of water is rainfall, which ultimately feeds all natural springs and underground water reservoirs. Some of this rainfall flows into the oceans by forming rivulets, then streams and rivers. Flora and fauna use some of it up right away. Some of it disappears into the depths of the earth and remains hidden for decades, even centuries, in underground reservoirs, or aquifers, as they are called.

"The proportion of water to land determines the amount of rainfall. So it's not surprising to find the world's greatest amount of rainfall around the Pacific basin, the world's greatest body of water, covering nearly one-third of the globe. Converted by and carried aloft on the warming rays of the sun and influenced by solar frequencies, the uncontaminated ocean water vapours around the Fiji islands, liberated from the salt, are lifted from the ocean upwards through the untainted atmosphere. These vapours condense and return to Earth as pristine raindrops. What happens from here creates the best drinking water on the planet—FIJI Water.

"The virgin rainwater … filters through a water-bearing formation of fragmented basalt rock, sandstone and other natural silicates within a 15-km diameter volcanic crater, some four to five million years old, located at the Yaqara Valley on the northern side of Viti Levu [the largest island of the group and the site of the international airport], then into an aquifer deep beneath the lush volcanic highlands and pristine tropical forest. Influenced by geomagnetic frequencies, this water becomes the 'lifeblood' of the Earth."

This, according to Hendel and Ferreira, is how the source of the world's best and most beneficial water is created: The unpolluted, uncontaminated, absolutely pure water descends from the sky, and then continues its gravitational descent down the mountains in waterfalls and crevasses, passing through fissures in rock, through sand, and through silica beds. It is during this process that the water picks up its silica dioxide, thereby taking on its distinctively soft taste and health benefits.

This is how the pristine, underground aquifer that is the source of FIJI Water got started. How I got started on FIJI Water is a little more down to earth. It began with a golf game.

FIJI Water, the company that I founded in 1997 and that I sold in 2004, began with a simple observation. Most of my start-ups do. With Clairtone, it began with my standing in a living room and looking at yet another ugly record player—and wondering why there couldn't be a beautifully-designed, high-quality alternative. With Thumper—a chiropractic massage vibrator developed by Dr. Ed Noble that I financed and put on the market in 1983—it was the simple observation that there had to be a way for people to do for themselves what chiropractors and masseuses did for them in their clinics. I'd had back problems myself, and Dr. Noble's idea of an efficient handheld device for deep therapeutic massage made sense to me. More than that, it worked on me, and so I encouraged him to leave his chiropractic practice and devote himself to perfecting Thumper. It is still widely used to this day—including by Jill and me.

All of these ideas had their origins in something my father taught me to hold in high regard: the art of paying attention to what is often right in front of us. With FIJI Water, my moment of revelation could hardly have been more ordinary—on the face of it.

One day, while I was playing golf with Jill, we stopped to allow a couple to play through. It was a lovely afternoon. We were enjoying our game and in no great hurry. Life has a calm, meditative pace in Fiji. A game of golf isn't something crammed between this appointment and that. A game of golf is allowed to be exactly what it is, and there is no reason to be impatient.

While we paused, I watched one of the players take a bottle of Evian from his golf bag. I considered this, and, as seems to happen frequently in Fiji, I found myself pondering this perfectly ordinary, perfectly everyday activity from a new perspective.

"Something is wrong with this picture," I said to Jill.

Jill looked at me as if I'd lost my mind. And I could see why.

From her point of view there was very little wrong with this picture. It was a gorgeous day. We were in a stunningly beautiful place. We were happy and healthy and blessed with good fortune. It seemed as if the picture was just fine, thank you very much. Rather hard to improve on, as a matter of fact!

But Jill gave me one of those looks. Husbands know the look I mean.

"Are the parrots too loud?" she asked. "Is the sky too blue or the clouds too white? Is the temperature too perfect? The gentle breeze too gentle? Are the rustling palm fronds making too much noise? Honestly, darling, what are you talking about?"

The world has always been full of things that don't make sense. We have learned to take them as a matter of course. But this seems particularly true of our troubled day and age. Experience and human nature point in one direction. Why, then, do politicians choose another? Obesity worries us as a society, so why do we open more and more fast-food restaurants? We watch business boom when we remove the obstacles that stand in the path of entrepreneurial enterprise; why do we regulate ourselves into a state of economic paralysis?

One doesn't have to do much more than watch the news for five minutes to witness the triumph of the nonsensical. And yet we seldom comment on it. We are completely inured to it. We hardly notice it anymore.

But for some reason, that day, as I watched a guest pull a bottle of Evian from a golf bag, the absurdity of consuming water from heavily populated, heavily industrialized, heavily polluted Europe while being in the pristine environment of the South Pacific really got to me. The more I thought of it, the more ridiculous it became.

As I explained my thinking, Jill's expression of bewilderment gave way to one of agreement.

"Within a hundred miles of here," I said to her, "I'll bet there is a beautiful artesian aquifer waiting to be discovered." And, as it happened, I was right.

It's not easy being a newcomer. In fact, it can be downright unnerving. The market FIJI Water was entering was dominated by beverage giants that had staked out their markets long before we came on the scene.

There were 620 bottled water companies in North America when we entered the fray, and the largest of them had advertising budgets that we could only dream of. Many of them were already long-established national or international brands with high name recognition and consumer loyalty. They had nailed down their distribution networks, and their products were familiar to store owners, to managers, to restaurateurs, to bartenders, and to consumers. However excellent our product—and I was certain that FIJI Water was, quite simply, the best drinking water in the world—I knew we had a very demanding game of catch-up to play. The task was daunting, to say the least. But with FIJI Water, as later with Zinio and Wakaya Perfection, I kept some wonderful advice my father once gave me firmly in mind: "Self-doubt undermines confidence, and without confidence, any project suffers, if not fails."

Armed with the kind of self-assurance that my father believed to be essential to business success, I eventually did what I should have done at the outset. I trusted my instincts and hired

Doug Carlson. By his own admission Doug knew nothing about consumer products. He had been managing the Aspen Club, which was where I'd got to know him. His experience was in the hospitality industry. His education was in accounting. He was not, on the face of it, an obvious choice. My instincts said otherwise.

When I interviewed Doug in my apartment in Paris—Jill and I were living there at the time—my last question was a bit of a curve: I asked whether he played golf. I wanted to have someone on board whose job, and not his handicap, was his focus. But golf is often thought to be a requirement for business, and I remember that Doug looked suddenly very dejected. He replied that he did not. I could see that although the answer was one he thought would work against him, he had told me the truth. This impressed me enormously. Perfect, I thought.

An example to the contrary was Doug's predecessor at FIJI Water. I felt uncertain about him from the beginning. There were one or two little alarms going off each time we spoke. But I was entering into an industry about which I knew very little. I made the mistake of thinking that his experience, coupled with my inexperience, outweighed my qualms about him. This proved to be an error in judgment—a departure from my own belief in my instincts.

I suppose I could say that he was simply incompetent. Every piece of equipment he purchased had to be discarded within two years. Or I could say that he had no marketing skills whatsoever. His idea of selling was to fill a sea container with product and essentially dump it in, say, South Korea. Product knowledge—information to be conveyed to distributors, to retailers, to restaurants—was not part of what he considered his job. Follow-up was an alien concept to him. In-store display was not his department. He seemed to think that the water would just sell itself—in contrast to the slow, steady creation of product visibility, trial, and consumer advocacy that became the hallmark of my success with FIJI Water. But really what stands out in my memory of his failures as a manager is that I heard him use the term "coconut heads" when speaking of our Fijian partners, colleagues, and employees. That was the last straw!

I was intent on building a partnership with our employed Fijians, of sharing the company's success with them and making them feel as if we were all working toward a mutually beneficial goal. As well, proceeds from FIJI Water were assisting with my establishment of preschools throughout the islands and a trust fund for the benefit of all Fijians. I wanted our company's pledge to "make a difference" to be more than a meaningless corporate phrase. I wanted FIJI Water to have a real impact on the lives of the Fijian people, and as far as I was concerned, the starting point of that commitment was respect.

My manager's disdain for our Fijian colleagues was not just rudeness or bigotry—although I have a low tolerance for both. His callous disregard for the native population was a clear signal that he simply was not on my wavelength. Not by a long shot. It was impossible to think the way he did and have, at the same time, the frame of reference that was so critical to what FIJI Water was all about. What experience he had in the industry was entirely beside the point. He had to go. When I confronted him with his self-inflicted business problems and with my strong objections to his racist slurs, he resigned, after begging me to buy back the stock options I had given to him.

Doug and I, on the other hand, were on the same wave-length. Almost immediately, we began talking about approaching our marketing in an entirely new way. Most beverage producers see their key relationship as being the one that they establish with their distributors. It is distributors who get the product into stores and restaurants; it is distributors who fight—or who do not—to make sure a product is displayed prominently. We decided to take a different approach. We decided that we wouldn't think of the distributor as our customer. The consumer would be FIJI Water's customer—and everything we did would flow from that.

I devised a marketing scheme that was much more intently focused on events than the kind of haphazard publicity of our competition. And we all worked hard to choose the right kind of prestigious, high-profile gatherings. We wanted celebrities to be seen with FIJI Water on their tables or better yet, in their hands. We also worked at marketing by means of what we called "neighbourhood niches"—looking at the lives of people in high-profile neighbourhoods in Palm Beach, Beverly Hills, and Aspen. We rightly predicted that if these people were seen with bottles of FIJI Water in their homes—or in their restaurants, or at their fitness clubs, or on the tables of their galas—then others would follow their example. And finally, we made sure our bottle—squared rather than round, and bearing a bright, distinctive tropical label that bespoke a unique quality, taste, and benefit—would stand out. As we always described the steps of our marketing plan, it was all about visibility, trial, and product evangelism. It was about creating a brand that dared to be different.

And there was another element to our unique marketing approach. It involved enlisting me as a salesperson. It was an approach to things—to selling and to life in general—that I had learned during my time in the army.

I am not a manager. I am a creator. It is the thrill of original thinking that creates value and wealth—and by definition, original thinking is forward thinking. For an entrepreneur, perhaps more so than for others, life is about tomorrow and not about today or yesterday. I am not very interested in reviewing the review of the review. I am not interested in poring over reports on reports. If a post-mortem comes as news to me, I am inclined to think I'm doing something wrong. I am interested in what works, and in what will work—and something that I learned in the army is that knowing things from the ground up is a good way to do just that.

When I joined the Horse Guards in 1951, I came from the kind of background that was assumed to be officer class. My upbringing was respectable, and my parents were highly regarded. As well, I was a university student. As a result, I got my commission. That was simply the way the system worked.

I was what was known as a "One Pip Wonder"—a second lieutenant, in other words. This rank was the lowest rung on the commissioned officer's ladder—the "pip" referring to the insignia on the shoulder of an officer, designating rank. And it was a proud day for me when, in the company of two fellow one-pippers, we first sidled up to the bar in the officers' mess in Toronto's armory on University Avenue.

Sadly, that fine old building was torn down in 1963. It seemed to me at the time that Toronto was turning its back on an enormously important part of its history when the wrecker's ball crashed into those red brick walls. In 1914 and then again in 1939, that parade ground had echoed with a command that changed the lives of thousands of men and that was emblematic of Canada's proud tradition of service: "Volunteers, one step forward." It has often been said that Canada became a nation on the battlefields of the First World War. If so, the first step toward that nationhood was taken in buildings such as the University Avenue armory.

It wouldn't have taken a great deal of imagination and money to have found ways to preserve the building and to have found other municipal uses for it. I think of this whenever I hear of one of the many private parties, art exhibitions, trade shows and antique fairs that are held in the New York City armory.

The destruction of the Toronto armory was an unnecessary shame. It seems to me now part of the disregard for history that inflicts such appalling ignorance on so much of contemporary life. "The further backward you can look, the further forward you can see," Winston Churchill said—and I often think that many of the social, political, and military difficulties we face today are the result of the kind of historical forgetfulness that great man was warning us against.

In her marvelous book, *Paris 1919*, Margaret MacMillan makes this point with absolute clarity. As I read, it became apparent why so many historians believe that the past is the most reliable tool we have for reading the uncertain tea leaves of the future. "Some of the most intractable problems of the modern world have roots in decisions made right after the end of the Great War," Professor MacMillan writes. "Among them one could list the four Balkan wars between 1991 and 1999; the crisis over Iraq (whose present borders resulted from Franco-British rivalries and casual mapmaking); the continuing quest of the Kurds for self-determination; disputes between Greece and Turkey; and the endless struggle between Arabs and Jews over land that each thought had been promised them." We turn our backs on history at our peril.

And yet the invaluable lessons of history are increasingly lost on our society, and not just on the uneducated. I was recently at a dinner party in New York City at which the subject of the Second World War came up. A woman—sophisticated, it appeared; educated, one could only assume—was holding forth, and although she was articulate and bright, I eventually became suspicious of her grasp of the past. "How many people do you think were killed in World War II?" I asked.

Her reply? "Oh, gosh," she answered. "Let's see. About 300,000?" I stared at her, dumbfounded. "Would you believe in excess of 50 million?" I said. I was so upset I'm not sure I heard her reply. It was an example of ignorance that I fear is a hallmark of our age. Knocking down the armory in Toronto was more than just demolishing an old brick building. The lessons of the past are lost on us because, increasingly, the past is not something we value or something we preserve.

In the 1950s in Toronto, the University armory still stood front and centre in the city's life. It was a grand, red-brick fortress of a place—a monument to the heyday of Toronto's Victorian architecture, and to the civic prominence once given to the military.

The officers' bar was exactly the burnished wood that you would expect, and the scene just as congenial. And there we were: three new one-pip-wonders rubbing shoulders with the captains, majors, and lieutenants of the regiment. The three of us were well pleased with ourselves—or rather, we were until we encountered the not-to-be-trifled-with countenance of Colonel Bud Baker.

Baker was the commanding officer of the regiment. He had piercing blue eyes and a twisting sarcastic grin that he liked to put to use when he was giving orders that he knew his men didn't want to hear. He was tough and plain-spoken, and he had an impressive war record. He'd fought with the regiment in Italy in '44 as it moved in pursuit of the German army up the boot of Italy. The fighting was vicious. Canadian casualties were heavy, and some of the battle stories told about Bud Baker were legendary. He was a soldier through and through: tough, blunt, practical. He was not at all the kind of officer who bothered to put much in the way of a question mark at the end of his sentence when he said to the three one-pip wonders: "Gentlemen. Could you step outside to the foyer, please."

Needless to say, we stepped outside to the foyer.

I'm not sure whether this was something he'd been stewing over for awhile. Or whether it was the sight of the three of us— young, inexperienced, and perhaps a little too smug—that had made him make up his mind. At any rate, Colonel Baker had decided that he'd had enough of officers being appointed by social introduction. "As of tonight," he said, "all men who become offi- cers must come up through the ranks." The choice was ours. We could get ourselves down to the basement, pick up a "troopers" uniform, and joint the enlisted men. Or we could go home.

I could see nothing wrong with the idea. In fact, it made sense to me. My father and my grandfather had both come up through the ranks. Alas, mine was a dissenting view. Of the three, I was the only one who made the trip to the quartermaster's store.

I probably couldn't have quite articulated my reasoning then, but I can see now that it fits with the philosophy I've developed in business over the years. I believe that it is important for execu- tives to know a company from bottom to top, for exactly the same reasons that Colonel Baker wanted his officers to come up through the ranks. If you're going to order someone to clean the oil filter of a Sherman tank when it's so hot and dusty you can hardly breathe, you can do so with conviction and with high expectation if you know that you could do it—indeed, have done it—yourself. This holds as true for corporations as for regiments. And this was why David H. Gilmour, Executive Chairman of FIJI Water, was the company's most dogged salesman. My team had decided that nobody could speak about FIJI Water with the knowledge and conviction I had. After all, it was my company. After all, I drank it religiously. And so I hit the road.

☥

I think the weaknesses of a corporation can often be caused by a rarefied executive—a class that is far removed from the nuts and bolts of what the enterprise actually is. That's why, when we were starting up FIJI Water, I spent days in the delivery truck. With my knees tucked up to my chin, I spent as many days in the compact cars of our sales reps. I wanted to personally introduce FIJI Water to as many variety store owners and mom-and-pop grocery shops as possible. (And that is why now, I make as many sales calls as possible for our Wakaya Perfection products. If I am not going to be a passionate representative of the remarkable benefits of my own products, who will be?)

The proprietors of these little establishments would have been bewildered, and probably embarrassed, had they been invited to some fancy function, or had some big limo pulled up to their front doors. But they were impressed when the owner of the company climbed down from a delivery truck to tell them why he believed so passionately in a product he hoped they would carry on their shelves. They were certainly impressed when, unlike the pop delivery men who simply handed them a delivery bill to sign, I introduced myself, showed them my card, and then opened a bottle of FIJI Water and passed it to them. "Please," I said, "have a drink." No one had ever done this before!

I knew that it was crucial for FIJI Water to gain visibility up and down the city streets of North America, and I had already decided that this would be accomplished under the radar of our competitors. There would be no national advertising campaign. Everything would depend on the axiom on which all my business ventures have been based: Visibility creates trial, which creates advocacy.

The best way I could see that happening was to employ Bud Baker's philosophy: I'd join the ranks. I'd get on the street, bottle of FIJI Water in hand. Store by store, shopkeeper by shopkeeper, restaurant by restaurant, tasting by tasting. I made sure that FIJI Water developed a strong, personal relationship with the people who would represent us to our customers. This was visibility. No amount of advertising could compare to the effect of the owner of a little variety store telling a regular customer that FIJI Water actually tastes better than Evian, better than Vittel—considerably better than the bottled tap water that is sold as "spring" water by some major brands. This was trial. If I were passionate about the product, which I was, my passion was the most important message I could convey to them. And that is what they, in turn, would pass on. They would become our evangelists and the consumers our converts. This was advocacy.

Fiji (THE WAKAYA CLUB & SPA)

THE POISON WEED

"A lie gets halfway around the world before the truth has a chance to get its pants on."
—Sir Winston Churchill

WAKAYA HAS A CHARACTERISTIC—SOMETHING IN THE AIR and the light—that I think of as corrective. No sooner am I back here than it feels as if everything has been realigned. Our guests often notice it, too. Here they find the ability to let the frantic pace of the world slip away, to calm down, and to see things in a new perspective. There have been instances of solutions being found here that were elusive in a more cluttered and stressful environment.

I think it's a matter of learning how not to bother with things not worth bothering about. There's too much beauty on Wakaya to devote much time to the inconsequential. This view from our deck—of the shifting dawn of sea and sky, of the canopy of trees revealed as the day slowly lightens—is too magnificent to be troubled by unimportant concerns. My experience is that pointless worries fall away naturally as I sit here and watch the day begin. It's a kind of meditation, I suppose.

The Wakaya effect is just as revealing in what doesn't

fall away—because even in the most beautiful places, there are sometimes domestic concerns, or social concerns, or business concerns, or political concerns that we carry with us for good reason. Wakaya is not an escape so much as it is an adjustment of perspective—and an adjusted perspective doesn't mean all the bad things simply go away. Wakaya has the capacity to winnow away trivial concerns, but as it does, it sometimes reveals the serious problems to be confronted—just as the dawn reveals the details of branch and leaf in the boughs of the trees I am looking over now.

Something I worry about—even here, so far from our residence in Florida and our pied-à-terre in Manhattan, and under the most ideal conditions imaginable—is what I see as the hypocrisy of public life in America. The sense that biases and the dictates of self-interest (always part of the cut-and-thrust of political life) have crossed a line into a new and frightening territory.

Capitalism is not always kind. But if you take the long view, capitalism is a system that by its very nature tests itself for quality, for efficiency, and, ultimately, for profitability in every transaction of every day. The great strength of capitalism is not that it rewards success—although I'd be the first to admit that it does. No, the greatness of capitalism is how mercilessly it passes judgment on failure. As a society we benefit from a simple rule of thumb that is all but unknown to socialism: We get rid of things that do not work in favour of things that do.

Free enterprise is the entrepreneur's environment: the place where innovation and the creation of wealth can intersect. But creative capitalism can only function in a jurisdiction in which the deepest respect for justice and truth underlies everything. Alas, I think we are approaching the place where this is no longer the case.

As much as I detest the demotivation of mankind by the transparent manipulation of the unmotivated and uneducated, I also fear that there is a present and growing danger of a very small minority among us destroying the financial system of capitalism by the sheer unmitigated and unrestrained greed of a few who are selling corrupt and unscrupulous products to unsuspecting governments and citizens of the world—or to people just like you and me. Unchecked, unmitigated avarice and greed are not fundamental traits of the capitalist system ... never have been and never should be.

I am often amazed at how things have changed in the world of politics. Today, for example, the former president is pilloried for going to war against Saddam Hussein in the belief that the Iraqi dictator had weapons of mass destruction. George W. Bush and his administration are universally denounced—and yet, Bill Clinton once looked me in the eye and said that, as a former president, he was privy to the same intelligence President Bush was receiving, and based on that, he would have made the same decision.

Today, many politicians spend one third of their time raising funds for the next election, another third avoiding the truth, and another dealing ineffectually with the people's business. In a country as great as the U.S., our priorities must shift back—and shift soon—to the fundamentals that, for so long, have encouraged American ingenuity and enterprise. Similar to my prognostication that the future is not about the disposable product, I also believe that the future holds no place for the disposable politician who cares only about the next financial reporting period and does not take the slightest amount of time to understand the intricacies of the system he or she has sworn to uphold and benefit! My fear and belief is that we are approaching a place where the truth is not honoured and where the playing field is not level. California—a state in which I will likely never do business again—may already be such a place. Let me tell you a story—I call it the story of the poison weed.

Moments after I had my revelation about FIJI Water on our golf course on Wakaya Island—after I'd convinced Jill that I was not entirely out of my mind about something being amiss in that otherwise utopian view—I felt a familiar twinge of excitement. Before I'd finished my golf game, the wheels were beginning to turn once more. And they kept turning. In what now seems like no time at all, I became passionately involved in establishing a state-of-the-art bottling plant and in marketing the pure, clear water of the Fijian rainforest that had found its way to the pristine aquifer hundreds of feet below ground.

However, as all entrepreneurs know, a good idea and a great product are only the first two steps on an often-challenging road. As I never tire of pointing out, "Luck, in the business world, is where preparation meets opportunity." But worries come with the territory, as well. Production and distribution, marketing and management—these were the kinds of things that I expected to be my preoccupations. These sometimes rough seas are where the excitement, and the risk, of a start-up lie.

What I had not anticipated—what took me completely by surprise and what, under different circumstances, might have sunk FIJI Water completely—was our company's near-fatal encounter with what passes for "just arbitration" in the great state of California. If you are doing, or thinking of doing, business there and you have not heard of Judicial Arbitration and Mediation Services (JAMS), you may want to pay heed to my sad tale.

When we started out, FIJI Water was not a big player in the bottled water market. As a result, we were not able to link ourselves initially with the largest national distributors. We were obliged to piece together a network of smaller distributors—some of whom proved to be energetic and committed partners. While others, to put it diplomatically, were rather less so.

I am sorry to report that our distributors in the San Francisco area—M.E. Fox and Company, Inc. and Couch Distributing Company, Inc.—fell into the latter category. As is often the case, our arrangement with them was a verbal agreement.

While sales of FIJI Water throughout the rest of our markets were climbing steadily, Fox's and Couch's numbers reflected an undeniable stagnation. Originally, I had been encouraged by the fact that both Fox and Couch were distributors for Anheuser-Busch, a company I admire and respect. But as time passed I became increasingly perplexed by their inability to ride FIJI Water's upward curve in most other markets in the country. And, with time, perplexity gave way to chagrin. I concluded that there was no reason why in Northern California a chain such as Safeway, by far the dominant retailer, should have been bucking a nationwide trend—except for the obvious one. We needed better distribution. In approximately one year, Couch had realized a cash-operating profit for us of $28,579 and Fox, $39,393. Be still my heart.

Had the rest of our network of distributors proven to be as slow-moving as Fox and Couch, FIJI Water would never have become the success that it did. As a young company, FIJI Water depended utterly on the advocacy of those who represented us to the independent stores and to the chains in which our customers and our potential customers would find us. This was not a role Fox and Couch ever took on. To put it bluntly, they didn't have the fire in their bellies that we needed. But their lacklustre performance was not the key reason we decided that, in order for FIJI Water to prosper and grow, it was necessary to part company with them. We might have been able to encourage them to do a better job (though frankly, I doubt it), but there was another factor involved, one that we could do nothing to alter.

In Northern California, as is the case throughout the United States, it is the chain stores that control the lion's share of the grocery market. Whether you are producing ketchup, breakfast cereal, TV dinners, or bottled water, you either do business with the chains or you don't do business! And most chains have a policy that requires producers to be able to get their product to all stores, and for obvious reasons. It would be confusing, to say nothing of irritating, for consumers to have to figure out which of the stores of a Northern Californian grocery chain carried FIJI Water and which ones didn't.

In Northern California we were unable to provide this kind of guarantee—which was the equivalent of kissing 30 to 40 percent of the market goodbye. With 21 territories to cover, we were only reaching 20, a number that fell to 19 when one of our distributors went bankrupt. Clearly, this was an untenable situation. And so, acting as any business would, and acting, in our view, entirely within the "at will" agreement with our distributors, we undertook to shift our working relationship to a distributor that could get our product on the shelves of all 21 territories.

Sadly, Couch and Fox did not see things quite as we did. Fifteen days after what should have been our final meeting with George Couch, we received a letter from him protesting our egregious act. He accused us of undercutting his "exclusive" arrangement with FIJI Water.

We, of course, saw nothing egregious about what we had done. It was a question of our company's survival. We were also surprised to learn that we had entered into an "exclusive" arrangement with Fox and Couch. Of crucial interest here is the fact that George Couch's letter made no reference—none!—to what would become the foundation of the case against us two months later when Couch and Fox sued us.

We felt confident that our position was a strong one. We believed that we had acted fairly and prudently, entirely within the accepted norms of the industry. We also believed that we had honoured the verbal agreement we had made with Fox and Couch.

The trial, however, would be technical in its details, and since we wanted the case to be judged on the realities of the industry and not by what we feared might be the emotional over-simplification of the case as presented by a smooth-talking lawyer to a jury that may or may not have a grasp of commerce and business, we proposed arbitration. Fox and Couch agreed. This, as things turned out, was a big mistake on our part.

☥

Arbitration has a long and, for the most part, credible history in the United States. The American Arbitration Association (AAA), for example, is a reputable public service. The AAA is a not-for-profit organization that has, since its establishment in 1925, assisted individuals, organizations, and corporations in resolving disputes. In situations where the law is reasonably clear and two parties are intent on finding a just and informed solution to a dispute, arbitration often makes perfect sense. Certainly, arbitration held strong appeal to us. In arbitration, there is no docket to be cleared before the wheels of justice can turn—no small matter when the energy of a growing young company is in danger of being squandered on endless legal wrangling. In arbitration there is no long queue in which litigants, lawyers, and witnesses, like the stranded souls in the film *Casablanca*, "wait, and wait, and wait."

However, the neutral mediators and arbitrators of organizations such as the AAA are, by no means, the only games in town. Whereas the AAA is not-for-profit, there are arbitration services, such as Judicial Arbitration and Mediation Services (JAMS) in California, that function as businesses, and this distinction makes them animals of an entirely different stripe. "The pay-for-justice phenomenon extends nationwide, generating hundreds of millions of dollars in business a year," wrote Eric Berkowitz in an article published in the *Los Angeles Times Magazine*. "But it's most prevalent in California, where a largely unregulated private system now handles more commercial cases than do the courts, according to some in the industry."

Still, we believed that our case was strong. We felt sure that the JAMS-appointed judge would consider the evidence we were able to put before him, and that he would base his judgment on accepted standards of the industry.

We obviously didn't quite understand the finer points of California justice. Of course, we had assumed that the facts of the case, as related to the court by our opponents, would bear some passing resemblance to what we knew to be true. Our naïvety, it now seems clear, knew no bounds.

Judges employed by JAMS as "neutrals" are either retired state court trial judges or U.S. district court judges. Ours had served for many years on the bench. Not that his experience did us much good.

"Irresistible temptation" might be too strong a term to explain the lure of JAMS to a senior judge, but if it is too strong, it's not too strong by very much. In the United States, judges are esteemed, honoured, and respected. They are not, however, particularly well paid, which was precisely where JAMS saw its opening.

Windstar cruises, lavish hotels, sumptuous hospitality suites that just happen to pop up at judicial conventions—such are the seductive recruiting tactics of JAMS. And once JAMS has a judge's ear, the message is compelling. On the bench, a judge might expect to earn somewhere in the vicinity of $137,000 a year—not much more than the most junior lawyer who stands before the court. But on the JAMS payroll, a judge's income would likely triple. Kids to put through college? A wife who deserves a first-class holiday? The longed-for sailboat? The desperately needed renovation? JAMS is often the right thing at just the right time for senior judges.

Benefits, perks, expenses, and the possibility of becoming a shareholder in a growing, successful business are all part of the package presented to potential JAMS "neutrals." In his article, Berkowitz writes of the "hundreds of judges who have abandoned the bench to enrich themselves by working in the private sector. Among them are four former California Supreme Court justices who settle disputes for arbitration companies that hawk them like merchandise."

The flaw in this system is that a JAMS judge can so easily be pulled in two directions: the need for justice and the need to make JAMS successful. The fact that "neutrals" are employed by a company that actively sells itself to potential clients is a far cry from the unbiased justice that Americans assume to be what underlies all trials—whether they be trials of litigation or arbitration. And it is JAMS' need to be profitable that is the devil's fingerprint. Nobody's faith in capitalism is more unshakeable than mine, but profit and impartiality are rarely comfortable bedfellows. That judges are active participants in the success of JAMS means that they have a vested interest in the company's success. And, in California, its success depends on keeping its biggest and most supportive clients happy—or, at least, happy enough that they return to JAMS.

The same shifting ground is true of the law firms that use JAMS. Forget the need for justice for the moment, and simply look at things from a business point of view. Consider this conundrum. Which lawyer should JAMS try to make happy: the lawyer they've never heard of and will likely never see again, or the lawyer from a firm that writes JAMS arbitration into all their contracts?

One of the reasons we had gone to arbitration was to avoid the dangers of the "hometown" jury. This was a serious miscalculation on our part. No matter how much a local jury favoured a "home team," it could not have been less fair than the systemic injustice we encountered. A perversion of justice would not be too strong a description. Our JAMS judge not only overlooked the evidence we tabled to prove that we were within our rights to terminate our relationship with unsatisfactory partners, he accepted the distributors' projections of the profits they would make over the next several years, were they to continue their association with FIJI Water. Not since a friendly commodities broker helped Hillary Clinton turn $1,000 into $100,000 almost overnight has reality been so resolutely ignored. The projections of Couch and Fox would have been laughed out of any boardroom in the country—but not, sadly, out of our JAMS courtroom.

Undermining all notions of common sense, JAMS agreed

with the claim that the termination of our working relationship was going to result in a $4 million loss for our former distributors. How $70,000 of relatively lacklustre sales could be turned into the boom of $4 million is a mystery. All I know is that had I not been in a position to survive a $4 million cash call, the upward trajectory of an energetic young company would have come to an abrupt halt. As I wrote to Steven Price, the President and CEO of JAMS, in December of 2004: "The $4,174,948 award that was recently imposed on FIJI Water … is blatantly appalling, untethered to the reality of how business is conducted in this country, and threatened the demise of a company that on October 27, 2004, received the Secretary of State's 2004 Award for Corporate Excellence from Colin Powell…. California has long been considered anathema for business and [the JAMS' decision] has done much to advance and confirm this insidious reality."

And it gets worse! When Mr. Couch told me, to my face, that it was his intention to make an example of FIJI Water (presumably so that other unhappy clients would think twice about going elsewhere), I realized that I was witnessing something more than a personal financial blow. I was in plain view of the stifling of free enterprise and the celebration of mediocrity. I should have known. I suppose my first clue should have been that when I asked to meet with Messrs. Couch and Fox, they suggested we meet in a boardroom of the JAMS office in San Jose. They seemed perfectly at home there. Indeed, they acted as if they owned the place. Which, in a way, they did.

I won't soon forget Mr. Couch's smooth and unpleasant smugness, nor will I forget the half-smile that flickered across Mr. Fox's very pleased face. For doing a job poorly—so poorly we had felt we had no choice but to terminate our relationship with them—they were about to end up with a $4 million windfall. Both of them looked like cats who had just swallowed canaries. I could only marvel that Anheuser-Busch continued to do business with companies so lacking in morality.

I've endured snipers in Lebanon and crooks in Iran. Like most businessmen, I've had the misfortune of running across liars and thieves in the course of my career. But I've never dealt with anything quite like the judicial arbitration system that exists in the state of California. Already it has woven its way deeply into the commerce and legal system of that state. A dear friend of mine, Dr. Don Vinson, the noted jury expert and former university professor, has been stung once by JAMS. And once was enough. He is careful never to cross paths with them again, but almost signed a car lease recently before noticing, in the small print, the proviso that "all disputes would be settled by JAMS." He crossed the line out, and signed the contract. And when, as he expected it would, the leasing company called to object to this change, he said, "Well, come and take the car then." The company backed down.

JAMS is a system that can be so transparently biased, and so profoundly un-American in its potential for injustice, I might not believe it really existed were it not for the fact that Couch's and Fox's combined profit of less than $70,000 had been transformed into a reward to them—for doing their job poorly—of $4 million. Not even Houdini could have conjured a sleight of hand of that dimension. Years after we appeared before a JAMS judge, I sometimes catch myself thinking that it was only a dream—or, perhaps more accurately, a nightmare populated with a cast of fat, slovenly vampires.

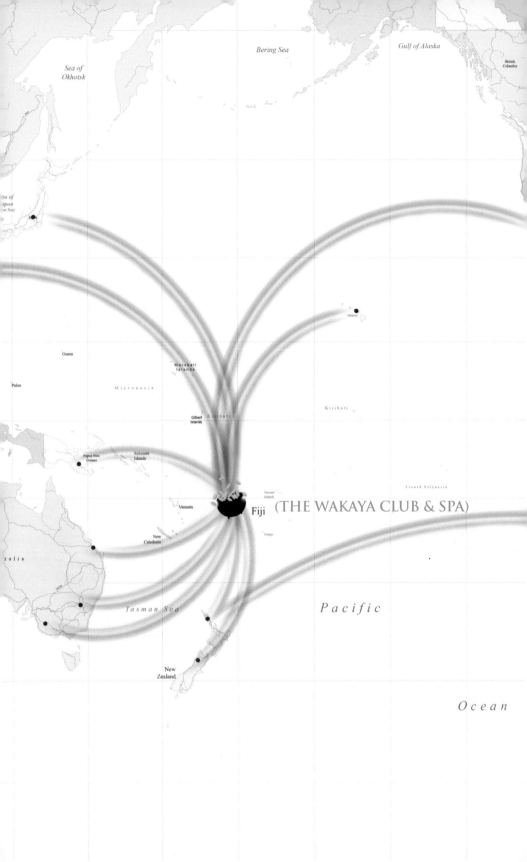

Fiji (THE WAKAYA CLUB & SPA)

GOING FORWARD

"The empires of the future are the empires of the mind."
—Sir Winston Churchill

SOME OF THE PEOPLE I NOW HAVE THE PLEASURE OF COLLABORATING with are not much older than I was when I went on my travels in Europe as a young man. They inhabit an exciting world—the world of computers, and smartphones, and e-readers, and apps, and clouds, and iPads. It is a world that is as young as they are, and just as full of promise. I have attended meetings at our offices in New York, San Francisco, and Barcelona and have left with my head spinning at the possibilities presented by digital publishing. What only a few years ago was a trickle of new technology is now a marketplace torrent.

When, at the age of 75, I became caught up in the plans for Zinio—working with a wonderful team of innovative engineers, editors, designers, and marketers—I found myself waking up totally energized by the challenges of a new enterprise. Peter Munk has said of me that I'm someone who, when I move from one phase of life or from one business venture to the next, I totally leave the old behind and totally embrace the new. "David will be able to speak of nothing but FIJI Water one year," Peter said. "The next time I see him, it's nothing but Zinio and rich media technology. And now it's Wakaya Perfection. When he opens one door, he closes another."

That's true. But not entirely true. In my view it's more of a necessary shifting of focus. I sometimes wonder if it isn't something that I learned from my mother when I watched her throw herself passionately and wholeheartedly into her opera roles. When she was preparing for Elsa in *Lohengrin*, she didn't forget about her roles in *Tosca* or *Tannhäuser*. She just didn't think about them because her mind—her entire being, in fact—was consumed with the attention she was paying to the role of Elsa. I think that starting a business requires this same kind of passion. It's not so much closing a door as paying full attention to the open one.

In many ways the past few years have been one of those strange interludes between old and new technologies. Like the periods when automobiles were described as "horseless carriages," or when retailers were uncertain if colour televisions would ever replace the tried-and-true black and white sets, or when Betamax and VHS were battling it out. Those of us who could see what was coming in the new digital age—or at least had an idea of what was coming—were frequently met with incredulity, particularly if we happened to be talking with people who had a vested interest in preserving their carriage factory.

Here I raise a word of caution for would-be entrepreneurs. And the word is: patience. It's never easy to convince people—

whether they are bankers, potential investors, or possible clients or customers—of something that either doesn't yet exist or that exists only in a preliminary form. This dislocation between an entrepreneur's vision and the world that exists is simply part of creative capitalism. People are always going to find ways to say no. I think of the Canadian banker who listened to Peter Munk's and my plans for Clairtone, and who turned us down for a loan with words that might well have been carved above the doors of many banks in those days: "There's many a slip between cup and lip." I think of Harold Honickman, the CEO of one of the largest soft-drink bottlers and distributors in the United States, who, when I outlined for him our plans for FIJI Water, advised us against launching. He told us that the field was already too crowded and that our product would never get off the ground. And I think of all the publishers of traditional magazines who listened to us talk about *VIV* and Zinio in the early days of my involvement, and who then politely showed us the door.

This kind of rejection is simply a matter of course to the entrepreneur, and those who are setting out with a new idea or a new product must simply brace themselves for the inevitable. Bitterness or anger cannot be allowed to prevail in such circumstances, for the simple reason that those who are unable to see an idea in its nascent form are sometimes happy to embrace it when the view has become a little clearer. After FIJI Water had become a success, Harold Honickman approached me following a speech I gave in New York. He shook my hand and very graciously said, "I was wrong. Against all odds, you made it work." Many of the publishers who, only a few years ago, listened to our descriptions of Zinio with barely disguised condescension, amusement, indifference, or incredulity are now bashing down our doors. What sounded a little crazy, frankly, not so long ago, now looks like the future. Of course, I gloat—a little. But gloating should always be a brief and private pleasure.

The Apple iPad was the tipping point. Over one hundred and seventy million have been sold as I write. In the next two to three years, 50 new instruments will be on the market, and we expect the price of many of them to drop to a little over a hundred dollars. E-readers, electronic tablets, and iPads will become as ubiquitous as smartphones. They will change reading books and magazines as dramatically as iPods changed listening to music.

People will be able to link their reading tablets to the screens on the back of seats of aircraft or to the widescreen television in a hotel room. Reading will take on all sorts of new forms and functions—while still, of course, maintaining the intimacy of sitting down to read a book or a favourite magazine—but in digital form. By 2015, 80 percent of reading will be digital, and much of this revolution will, I believe, be led by companies like Samsung that have a clear and uninterrupted view of the technological future. What an exciting time in the magazine business!

My own passion for magazines started at age 16, when I travelled extensively and alone for ten years. Magazines became a substantial part of my education. They became important building blocks, as I found they contained the essential sources of information and knowledge for me to build what became my career.

Emerging trends, economics, politics, fashion, health, travel, ecology, current events, human behaviour—these were the themes that magazines explored, and these were the areas of interest that, one way or another, would become professional preoccupations.

Now with the advent of the digital age both *VIV* and Zinio were created from a vision of becoming the global leader in what I refer to as the new reading revolution. An innovation of staggering implications that can be compared, without exaggeration, to Johannes Gutenberg's invention of moveable type 500 years ago. Magazine content is now completely portable and can be delivered instantly to any place in the world. With digital editions, magazines can be enhanced by rich, interactive content, resulting in vivid, immersive user experience. For advertisers, the digital revolution creates the possibilities of interactive capacity, layered depths of text and information, and (the holy grail of marketing) the ability to track with complete accuracy an ad's effectiveness and reach.

For these reasons—and, I hasten to add, because this is all so much fun—I am convinced that we are on the brink of a new golden age of publishing.

The world is changing with astonishing speed. I am now surrounded with people who have grown up "digital," and I can't help but feel that I have a ringside seat for the reading revolution. Zinio now distributes over 5,000 magazines globally. Recently, when one of our clients, *Rolling Stone* magazine, devoted an issue to the 500 greatest songs of all time, the magazine's association with Zinio made it possible for *Rolling Stone* subscribers to read about the songs online, and to hear them!

I'm not sure that we have ever witnessed a better generational fit than the digital age and the quick, bright, youthful minds that are at its forefront. The creativity and innovative spirit of my new colleagues reminds me constantly of what it was like to be their age. To be curious, to be open, to be ready to follow the unexpected turns that life presents.

These characteristics are also qualities that entrepreneurs must guard against losing as they grow older, for there is no such thing, really, as a staid, comfortable, set-in-his-ways creator of wealth. What entrepreneurs do is largely a matter of instinct, and if instincts become blunted with routine, if imagination becomes dulled by convention, and if potential becomes restricted by regulation, the way forward becomes not the way forward at all, but a way to stand still, to mark time, to tread water. To stay comfortable, perhaps, but not to move, not to experiment, not to make unexpected discoveries. Sometimes, in my gloomier moments, I wonder if our politicians simply do not understand the importance of encouraging and freeing up this momentum. Sometimes I wonder if misguided policies aren't beginning to undermine America's great restless energy—its youthfulness and its spirit of innovation.

Art historians, when they are called upon to verify the authenticity of a masterpiece, often speak of the moment of instant recognition. Bernard Berenson said that he knew at once if a painting was or wasn't by the artist in question, and that all that followed his initial, instinctual response was just gathering evidence to support what he already knew. This subconscious assimilation of data is similar, I think, to what I described earlier in these pages as the much underestimated entrepreneurial hunch. And while I don't compare myself to someone as learned as Berenson, I can't help but think that entrepreneurs have similar moments. Flashes of inspiration. Instants of understanding. Hunches.

Somehow I knew that the path that became Clairtone, and the path that became FIJI Water, and the path that has become Zinio and Wakaya Perfection were paths for me to follow. There were a thousand other routes that I might have taken, but somehow I knew that these were the directions I needed to take.

The ability to see a path before the path even exists confirms for me the belief that entrepreneurs and young people are really travellers—and, like travellers, they need to be adaptable to what the road brings to them. Otherwise, they won't learn anything. Otherwise, they won't create anything new. Otherwise, they might as well have stayed at home.

VIV was a totally new concept in women's magazines, and as such, was our test kitchen for the possibilities Zinio was exploring in the industry at large. Still, it was much more than an experiment. It was the first of its kind—the magazine of the future.

I've always been drawn to women's magazines—have always

thought, in fact, that their importance has been badly underestimated. I don't see the pursuit of a balanced, healthy lifestyle as being in any way trivial. Quite the opposite.

Women's magazines have always fascinated me. Far from being the "lightweights" of the business that the so-called "heavyweights" often make them out to be, I have always seen them as extremely influential and important publications. All my life, whenever I've boarded a plane, a train, or a ship, I've taken a bag of magazines, several of which have been women's magazines, to pore over. Because I think of myself as a trendsetter or perhaps a tastemaker—someone who, in order to make sound and profitable business decisions needs to anticipate societal change—I've found magazines such as *W, Vogue,* and *Elle* to be enormously instructive—far more so than most men's magazines.

Their usefulness in providing me with a sense of trends in the making has only increased in the last several decades as the role women play in all aspects of life continues to expand. I remember, by way of generational contrast, that my father presided over household expenses without consultation with anyone. There were occasions, when things were going well, when he would suddenly appear—with a new car! "Come out and see what I've got," he would say—and this would be a complete surprise to all of us, including Mother.

Such male domination of household finances—to say nothing of the choice of make, model, and colour of a purchase as significant as an automobile—would be totally unheard of today. Politically, socially, and economically, the transformation since my father's time has been extraordinary. Today, there are few married men who would take it upon themselves to go out and buy a car with no discussion with their spouses. Women are responsible for fully 80 percent of all purchases in America, and there is nothing lightweight about that. As well, women's use of home computers is rising by 20 percent per year.

All of which made *VIV* make sense in terms of a test kitchen and an entity of its own right for its time. To be blunt, America would be much better off if more of its citizens, male and female, made a quest for the kind of balance *VIV* espoused a bigger part of their lives. As Zinio began to grow and prosper, we made the decision to wind down the *VIV* enterprise, since its existence has accomplished all I wanted from it—and had in many ways paved the way for the interactive digital magazines that now make up the core of Zinio.

My association with *VIV* and Zinio has been rejuvenating—a fact I raise with some hesitation, only because an older man's quest for youthfulness is so easily turned to cliché. I hate to try to guess how many older men have told younger women, "You make me feel 18 again." I doubt there is a more overused line in existence. Nonetheless, that's the way working with my colleagues at *VIV* and Zinio has made me feel. I get to feel young—without feeling like a damn fool, the morning after!

In the fall of 1951, I was out for my last hurrah as a young, footloose traveller in Europe. I could sense responsibility and ambition waiting in the wings, but before I ushered them onto my stage, I wanted one last youthful adventure. My budget was precisely what the title of the popular old travel book said it should be. Europe on ten dollars a day.

The devastation of the war that I had seen on my trip to Europe in 1948—the leveled cities, the poverty and sad wasteland of unemployment, the meagre goods, was still apparent. The cost of war was obvious and staggering.

But things were being rebuilt, not, so I like to point out to my left-wing friends, by Russia or by worldwide socialism. Things were being rebuilt by America—by American capitalism.

And what was America's motivation in this mammoth reconstruction? Ruthless greed? Unalloyed self-interest? Certainly, those were the suspicions voiced by European leftists. It was pointless to try to argue that doing-the-right-thing might have had something to do with America's role in rebuilding Europe.

Well, whatever it was, it seemed to work. Thank God for Yankee imperialism! Hurray for the running dogs of capitalism! Three cheers for the almighty greenback! There was a strong sense of optimism in the air in Europe in 1951, a mood that rather splendidly accorded with my own youthful high spirits. It was a phenomenal time to travel. Ten dollars went a long way in Europe in those days.

I went to Paris and established my base camp for $2.40 a day in the attic of the Hotel Jacob, on the Rue Jacob on the Left Bank. In a letter to my father in which I rendered a detailed accounting of my daily Paris expenses (Food: $3.15; Transport:

$1.20), I noted that I could have taken a less expensive room, but it would have been a room without windows. I had decided to splurge on air and a little light in the attic.

Even so, my digs were more a dormered closet than a room. My space was furnished by a narrow bed, an old chair, and a sink that I suspected generations of tenants had peed in rather than brave the chilly hallway that led to the rudimentary, very French toilet. If you looked up the word "garret" in the dictionary, you may well have seen a picture of my Paris pied-à-terre. Still, I couldn't have been happier.

"It is just the end of my first week in Paris," so I wrote to my parents, "which I have spent walking every street, rain or sun, night or day, and at last I feel I understand as well as know Paris. To be not a visitor but a friend."

One of the places I enjoyed spending time was the famous Café de Flore on the Boulevard Saint-Germain. It was celebrated as one of the meeting places of the French intellectuals of the day. Sartre, Simone de Beauvoir, and Albert Camus were often at its tables during the occupation. After the war, you might have seen Jean Seberg, Jacques Tati, Marcel Carne, Brigitte Bardot, Yves Montand, Alberto Giacometti, or Simone Signoret on its terrace. A favourite spot of Hemingway's, of Truman Capote's, of Arthur Koestler's and Lawrence Durrell's, it was popular with Parisians and expats alike.

Paris, in those golden days, was a paradise of fresh baguettes, delicious cheese, beautiful girls, inexpensive wine, and an excellent exchange rate. It was a city that was particularly popular with the GI Bill of Rights fellows—all of whom seemed to be studying art, or language, or writing—or French girls. The café life, the galleries, the nightclubs, the theatre made the city an extraordinarily exciting place to be—even on a budget, so my strictly-kept accounts reveal, of $7.45 a day.

Paris was also extraordinarily noisy. Cars were every-where, gridlock was endemic. Before the anti-honking laws were introduced, Parisians leaned on their horns when things weren't moving as quickly as they would like. Which was almost all the time, so far as I could tell while sitting, immobile, in backed-up traffic in the little Volkswagen convertible I'd bought in my first week.

Everybody thought they wanted to be a Hemingway and write the great American novel or, at least, they wanted to look as if that's what they were doing. And one of the best ways to fit in—to look as if you were perfectly at home, doing what people were supposed to do in Paris—was to sit at one of the side-walk tables at the Café de Flore, sipping an espresso, smoking a Gitane, watching the world go by. Which is exactly what I was doing, when one day, to my total astonishment, a prosperous, rather flamboyant-looking American came up to me and asked me if I'd like a job.

"Short term?" I asked. I wanted to keep my priorities straight. He said he was a movie producer. And as improbable as it sounds, it turned out that he was telling the truth. He was making a movie, and apparently he had just lost his leading man. He stared at me closely. I returned his inspecting gaze with what I intended to be the placid hauteur of youth. He said, "You know, you remind me of a young John Wayne."

I'd been told before that I looked like the young Alan Ladd, a resemblance I played up as much as possible with my proud ownership of a trench coat very similar to the one Ladd wore in *This Gun for Hire*. And now it was the young John Wayne? Well, who was I to argue? He was the movie producer. I was the penniless flaneur. He said, "Why don't you come over to the George V Hotel at five o'clock for an audition?"

I thought that this sounded like a lark. Exactly the kind of thing that was supposed to happen to you if you sat long enough in cafés in Paris looking artistic. And so later that day I fired up my trusty VW, and off I went.

I don't think the film was destined to win the Palme d'Or at Cannes. But I got the job. It was a caper-and-chase kind of story, and the filming was going to be done in seven or eight capitals of Europe, with shooting beginning in Rome. I was to play opposite a gorgeous model from the house of the celebrated couturier, Jacques Fath. We were to be newlyweds, being chased from luxurious hotel to chic restaurant, in some kind of detective whodunit.

And even better news, there was pay. Surviving on $10 a day was not a terrible hardship in France in the early 1950s. It was possible to get a very decent meal on the Left Bank for the equivalent of $2. But I certainly had no objection to improving my standard of living. And here was my chance. I was going to be paid $200 a week for a five- or six-week shoot.

The job would entail travelling, working with a beautiful model, and getting paid. You won't be surprised to learn that I accepted these terms. However …

The night before my career as a movie star was to begin, I went to a ball given by the Princess Polignac in Bois de Boulogne. Paris was famous for these grand, sumptuous parties—a rich tradition that brought together the city's bohemians and socialites. Man Ray and Horst might have been taking pictures and Picasso, Baba de Lucinge, the Duchess de Gramont, Cecil Beaton, Princess Natalie Paley, Daisy Fellowes, Cocteau, and Chanel might have been strolling through the throng. Invitations to these soirées were greatly coveted.

Through my sister Shelagh, who had been married to the head of Esso Norway, I'd made contact in Paris with the André family. Monsieur André was the head of Esso France. Wouldn't you know, Monsieur and Madame André had a lovely daughter, about my age, and it was she who had invited me to a dance that was one of the most exclusive of the social season. Just my luck!

It was a glamorous affair. It was at Les Trois Dauphins, and all of Parisian society was there. European aristocrats, American socialites, the young and beautiful, the old and rich, the movie glitterati. There was Doris Duke. There was Gerard Philippe. And there was the famous playboy, Porfirio Rubirosa. (To this day, waiters in Paris call the large wooden pepper grinders Rubies, in recognition of that fabled part of his anatomy that played some considerable role, so I can only assume, in his marriages to a number of extremely wealthy heiresses.)

As I watched le tout de Paris dance the night away, it certainly felt to me as if I wasn't in Kansas—or Toronto— anymore. My expectations of the City of Lights were by no means modest, but already Paris was exceeding them. At four o'clock in the morning, flying high with the excitement of the night (but totally sober), my date and I were I driving down the Champs-Élysées on our way home. I was in no rush to have the evening end, and so I was driving at a more than reasonable pace. I was approaching Fouquets—relishing the romance of being on the Champs-Élysées with a beautiful girl beside me. This was the life, I thought—even though I was certainly the only man who had been at Les Trois Dauphins that night who was driving his date home in a Volkswagen!

The Champs-Élysées was made of cobblestones in those days. They were glistening in a light rain. I didn't have a care in the world—until, three blocks below Étoile, as I made my way toward La Place de la Concorde, a truck suddenly pulled out of a side street to my left. It was a Citroën lorry, entirely in the wrong; I was entirely in the right. But the legalities of the situation were cold comfort at the time. I hit the truck broadside. Whoever the fool was who coined the famous aphorism, "What doesn't kill you only makes you stronger," had obviously never banged his head through the window of a Volkswagen.

When I came to, we were surrounded by a crowd of people—none of whom would help us. This was not, so I later learned, mean-spiritedness. It was collateral effect of the French legal system—one of those examples of Gallic philosophy and jurisprudence that leaves North Americans scratching their heads or, as in my case, trying to staunch its bleeding. Had they helped us, they would likely have been called to appear in court, which was a real catch-22 for French citizens. They had no option but to go to court. Their employers, on the other hand, had no obligation to allow them to. People often lost their jobs because they had to appear as witnesses.

Miraculously, and happily, my date was uninjured. (A few days later when I inspected my much banged up car, I saw, on the inside of the passenger's windshield, a perfect outline of lipstick, and between the lips, an inch-long cut in the glass. Somehow she had not so much as even a chipped a tooth.) Eventually an ambulance arrived, and we were taken to the American hospital in Neuilly where I was denied entry because I was a Canadian. This seems amusing now, if only because Canadians are almost always taken for Americans no matter how much they protest— but not so amusing then. Nobody knew quite what to do with me it seemed, so we were taken to a police station.

About all I can remember is lying on the floor of the station with someone's knee on my chest while someone else wielded an alarming looking stitching needle. They gave me the rag of a mop to bite on, making me feel as if I'd been wounded at the Battle of Waterloo. They sewed my face up. An excellent job, considering my surgeon was a constable. They seemed very accommodating, at first. There was no shortage of volunteers to drive my pretty date to her home on the Avenue President Wilson.

But here the hospitality of the gendarmerie ended. I was not feeling particularly steady on my feet, but my request that I be driven back to my hotel was greeted with the disdain for which the French police were so well known. "What do you think we are? A taxi service?" asked one of the officers. And so, still in my dinner jacket, I was required to walk from the Bastille to the Rue Jacob, as dawn was breaking over Paris. I had my passport, but no money. At some point during my misadventure, some good Samaritan must have taken it upon himself to relieve me of my cash.

Under other circumstances, this might have been a pleasant walk. Paris, as I know from more pleasant experiences, is an excellent city in which to stay up all night. Its beauty is often revealed most clearly to home-bound revelers in the secret moments between night and day. Unfortunately, my timing was terrible. I was neither looking nor feeling very well, and, to make matters worse, the city was preparing for its May Day celebrations that morning. Leftist students and workers were already in the streets, getting ready for a day of parades and demonstrations, and there was I, in dinner jacket, wending my way home on foot. I looked for all the world like the very model of the decadent, spoiled capitalist after a night of wild and socially irresponsible behaviour. I got more than a few dirty looks from passers-by. I'm amazed that nothing more befell me as I staggered toward the Hotel Jacob.

Eventually, I climbed the six floors to my room. A Himalayan peak would not have been a more difficult ascent. I was too exhausted to undress. I collapsed on top of my narrow bed.

And there I was—still dressed and sound asleep—when the movie producer found me. He'd come around, as planned, bright and early, to pick me up.

He was not at all amused. Nor was he in any way sympathetic. And even though my sad state was no fault of mine, I could see why he would be put out. We were supposed to be on our way to Rome. I was to have been the star.

He stared at me in disbelief. I was giving a very good impression of someone who had been out on a terrible bender the night before.

He assessed my condition: bandages, stitches, cuts and scrapes. More Boris Karloff than John Wayne. Then he threw up his hands in exasperation, swore once or twice, and left. And thus ended my career as a movie star.

The beautiful actress Arlene Dahl once said to me with grave certainty that I could have become an actor. I am reluctant to disagree with the opinion of such a gracious and perspicacious woman. But to tell you the truth, I'm not so sure. I suspect now what I did not allow myself to consider as a possibility when I was a young man in Paris: I was probably a terrible actor.

I've known a few very good actors quite well, and I've learned that an actor's remarkable talents are utterly distinct from mine. There is one role I play quite well—me. An ability to act has never been a tool that I have been able to put to use in my business life. I am incapable of pretending to be enthusiastic about a product in which I don't believe. Fortunately, I've never had to demonstrate my inadequacies as a thespian. Clairtone, FIJI Water, *VIV*, Zinio, The Wakaya Club and Spa, Wakaya Perfection—I've believed wholeheartedly in them all.

I find it revealing, though, that the lost opportunity to act did not break my heart. Even as I was listening to the angry producer stomp down the stairs from my room in the Hotel Jacob, I felt a certain calm acceptance of what the fates had given me. Being denied something is a good way to learn where your true calling lies.

In other words, the work has to be what you most want, not the results of the work. The truck on the Champs-Élysées was, in the long term, not such a bad twist of fate for me. I was upset because I'd lost that vast sum of money I was going to be paid. I was saddened because I'd rather enjoyed youthful daydreaming about the prospect of becoming a celebrity. And I was deeply, deeply depressed at missing so golden an opportunity to spend some quality time with that beautiful Jacques Fath model who was to be my co-star. But I can see now that it was just as well. Even had that lorry not struck my poor old Volkswagen, I doubt I would have seen my role in that film as anything more than the youthful lark that it was. I didn't have the fire in my belly to be an actor. I would take an entirely different direction.

The world of motion pictures got along just fine without me. And I got along quite well without it. The path I ended up taking turned out to be the one I was meant to be on. It's a path that has twisted and turned unpredictably, but that has led me, 60 years later, to where I am now. How could I possibly complain about that? Even if I do sometimes wonder wistfully whatever became of that beautiful model.

When people say that I am a romantic, I always make a point of correcting them. I see no contradiction between being a dreamer and a businessman. After all, it was no less of a pragmatist than Eleanor Roosevelt who said, "The future belongs to those who believe in the beauty of their dreams." If by business you mean the creation of wealth and not only its management, I'd argue that dreaming is the essential ingredient. "I am an incurable romantic," I say—for the simple reason that it is the romantics, the dreamers, who ask the question that others do not.

Why not? It's a question on which mankind has thrived. And it's a question that reaches back to the very first step I took in the world of marketing. When I was a young man, selling pots and pans door to door in Montreal, I realized that I would best be able to convey the quality of my product to prospective customers through demonstration. But I couldn't very well make dinner for them, could I? And that was when a lightbulb went on in my mind: Why not? I began making dinners for my potential customers—in their own kitchens—and I ended up selling lots of pots and pans as a result.

Not many years after that I asked the same question about record players. They couldn't be beautifully designed, could they? Why not?

The entrepreneur comes up with an idea, develops the idea, creates a plan to support the idea, finds the financing to support the plan, and then brings the original idea to reality. It is a process that I love dearly. I thrive on it, frankly. It was what gave me such a kick when, in 1997, I set out to turn FIJI Water into a successful national brand. And it's what is giving me such a kick now in the digital, "rich media" world that Zinio is helping to open up. It is a characteristic of youth to be looking to the future, but that is what, even at my age, I spend my time doing now, because I am utterly convinced that the traditional forms of printed magazines and newspapers are in the process of extraordinary reinvention. Already, even members of my own generation— people who once insisted that a computer screen would never replace the printed page—are admitting that they are getting more and more of their news and information online. Already, they are realizing that travelling with an iPad is infinitely more convenient than lugging around a suitcase full of books and magazines. The times are indeed changing. In fact, I'm not sure that in the history of mankind they have ever changed as much as they are changing now. Now, when I come to Wakaya for one of our stays, instead of suitcases of books and magazines, I have everything I want to read—and more!—in a tablet that weighs less than my shaving kit.

It was only a few years ago now that I was standing in our New York apartment one Sunday morning, and I was contemplating the economic meaning of the vast pile of newsprint before me. It was a familiar feeling. Much like the revelation that befell me in Fiji when I watched a golfer pull a bottle of European water from his bag—a revelation that eventually gave birth to FIJI Water—I found myself staring at the Sunday *New York Times* and thinking: There is something wrong with this picture.

Had Jill been present, she might have expressed exactly the same bewilderment that she had on the golf course in Fiji. Was our apartment not comfortable enough? Was our view of Manhattan not good enough? Was a Sunday in New York City— with a morning to sip coffee and read the paper and perhaps, later, go for a walk in Central Park—not a delightful enough prospect? Something was wrong with this picture?

Really? What exactly?

I'm not sure I knew myself at first. How many hundreds of times had I picked up other Sunday editions of the same paper without any troubling questions arising? But for some reason, on that particular Sunday morning, I found myself staring at that impressively thick pile of newsprint—most of which I had no interest in reading—and, for the first time, asking myself if it made sense.

The Sunday *New York Times* is a thick newspaper. (There are times when the conservative in me feels that it is thick in both senses of the word.) I used to think its size was exemplary of the abundance of American journalism, although in the back of my mind there was always Winston Churchill's famous quip about American newspapers being too thick and American toilet paper, too thin. But in recent years, I began to wonder if this wasn't rather less of a blessing than I'd thought. Then, on that fateful day, in our apartment in New York, I found myself simply staring at the Sunday edition. Ten or 12 sections—only three or four of which I was interested in opening. It seemed to me likely that this ratio would be far from a rarity among the Sunday paper's subscribers. An imbalance between production and consumption that struck me as totally inefficient. And wherever there is inefficiency, or waste, or a failure of imagination, there is always room for the observant entrepreneur to find a way to make the necessary—and often profitable—correction.

Still, there are times when the purpose is more than profit. There are times when the dynamics of capitalism can become the dynamics of necessary change. There are times when an idea can do more than make money. In this particular instance, it can be the force that might turn the rudder of a monstrous supertanker before it lands us all on the reefs of economic and environmental catastrophe. The real revolution at hand is not about cutting back, as so many of the Greens attest. It's about inventing new ways to do things. As Marshall McLuhan once said, "Our age of anxiety is, in great part, the result of trying to do today's jobs with yesterday's tools."

I wondered: What is the cost of producing one edition of this newspaper? I wasn't talking about the editorial cost. I was talking about the cost—both in dollars and in environmental expense—of the raw material of a newspaper's delivery system. I was wondering about newsprint. And the cost turns out to be staggering.

I am not exactly a Green Party member. The left-wing agenda of many environmentalists doesn't inspire confidence.

Anyone who is active is, to varying degrees, involved in the business of creating wealth—it's why I always make my employees shareholders in my projects. We are all in the business of making things better, smarter, more imaginative and efficient. Are computers so much better now than they were 20 years ago because computers have some kind of ingrained tendency to get better? Can you get a better cup of coffee on almost any street corner in an American city because coffee was going to improve on its own accord? Are we watching DVDs on wonderful home entertainment units instead of peering at a fuzzy signal on a black and white television because of some natural process of evolution? No. Our lives have improved because someone saw that there was money to be made by improving things.

The same will prove to be true when it comes to making our lives more efficient and less wasteful. Environmental responsibility is now a necessity—no one can deny that—and so there will be money to be made from it. This progress is where profit lies—and profit, contrary to what the left wing tells us, is what drives things forward. Efficiency, conservation, and sustainability are tenets of sound business practice. More than anyone, conservatives abhor unnecessary waste.

Sixty-four acres of trees are sacrificed for a single edition of the Sunday *New York Times*. That's one of those facts that, once you take it on board, pretty much says it all. The more I thought about these things, the less sense they made.

And once I began to wonder about newspapers, I found myself even more troubled by the mountains of magazines, unsold and unread, on display in the hundreds of corner newsstands throughout the city. Again, from a simple, businessman's perspective, I couldn't see how the industry made sense. From logging, to transportation, to pulp production, to printing, to distribution, and, finally (and often totally unused), to disposal—the production and delivery of magazines seemed to me to be based, to an extraordinary and totally insupportable degree, on inefficiency. My research revealed that magazines alone—not counting catalogues, not counting direct mail brochures and flyers—are responsible for the harvesting of 35 million trees a year.

There is a magazine store not far from where we live in Manhattan—International News, just off Columbus Circle—and I have to confess I made a bit of a nuisance of myself as I pestered the manager with my questions. It's always been my instinct to try to understand an industry at the point where the rubber meets the road. So instead of speaking to executives of giant publishing companies, I spoke to the guy in a store that sells newspapers and magazines, and it was at that level that the industry makes the least sense of all. Among the many startling facts I learned was this: International News carries over 6,000 titles. An impressive fact. Now be prepared to be really impressed. Fully 70 percent of all the magazines International News stocks are returned, unread and unsold, to their distributor. Seventy percent!

I found this totally bizarre—an indication of an industry that was based, to a great extent, on smoke and mirrors. If anything is truly unsustainable, an industry that throws away 70 percent of what it produces is surely that. And so, after noticing and then thinking about the products—the fantastically costly products—available on the newsstands of our neighbourhood in New York City, the idea for *VIV* began to take shape.

There is nothing easy about going up against the traditions of an entrenched industry. Just because 9 billion of the 12 billion magazines that are printed on paper in the U.S. annually are sent to landfills or are incinerated; just because the annual production of magazines produces 13 billion pounds of greenhouse gases and 4.9 billion pounds of solid waste; just because 70 percent of magazines sent to newsstands and retail outlets return to the waste stream unsold and unread; and just because 90 percent of all magazines are discarded within a year of publication—just because all this damning evidence is but the tip of a very unsustainable iceberg, does not mean the established magazine industry is not made up of some very stiff competition.

When I acquired Zinio, the software company that will allow us to capitalize on the enormous potential to which our test kitchen, *VIV*, so clearly pointed, I was convinced that there has to be a better way to communicate, entertain, and educate. Take the Victoria's Secret catalogues (all three million of them) as just one small example. To have these catalogues produced and delivered by the kind of "rich media" technology that Zinio is mastering is not only a great boon to the environment, it provides Victoria's Secret with marketing and advertising possibilities that have previously been unimagined. Want to see what a negligee looks like in red rather than black? Click here. Want to see a peignoir from a different angle? Click here. Want to order a pair of pajamas online? Click here. The possibilities are endless. Can you imagine the impact on advertisers when, simply by counting the hits on an online ad, they can know—know, not guess—how effective an ad is?

Zinio represents a new advance in the digital revolution. (In 2011, *VIV* won first prize as the best digital magazine in America. It won second prize for the best digital magazine in Europe—and while I'm not complaining, I can't help but wonder if *VIV* were a European magazine, and not American-based, would it have taken home first prize?) The revolution is radical, and yet it is entirely grassroots. It might change everything— from how we read, to how we communicate, to how we sell, but the public—so I sense—is ready for what is to come. Anyone who has ever asked a child or grandchild for assistance with a computer or a cell phone or an iPod knows that my generation's resistance to this kind of change is dissolving in the wake of the younger generations' enthusiastic embrace of what for them is not change at all. "The old world is rapidly aging," as Bob Dylan said. And make no mistake: No world is aging more rapidly than the way magazines used to be published.

Just as the public is famously ahead of politicians on environmental issues, so the public senses that the wasteful and unimaginative production of unread magazines, catalogues, and books cannot continue. I would guess that one of the most common complaints from households in America today concerns the unwanted flyers, catalogues, freebie magazines, and give-away newspapers that keep piling up on our doorsteps. I am suspicious of generalities, particularly generalities that have to do with national traits, but I think this holds generally true: Americans are practical people. They have an instinctive distrust of things that don't make sense. And, with the possible exception of the economic policies of the Democrats, nothing makes less sense than the old, outmoded magazine, brochure, and catalogue publishing business.

Nobody asks for this enormous pile of paper. More to the point, nobody wants it! And even more to the point, we can no longer afford it. It is not an effective or cost-efficient means of communication. Obviously, things are going to change. They have to!

I see the technology that Zinio is exploring as a real sea change. In this exciting world I recognize the thrill of doing what I've been fortunate enough to do over and over throughout my life: start something new. The excitement of *VIV* and Zinio have made me feel much the same as I did when, more than five decades ago, I set out on the course that has brought me to where I am today. Each day brings a new set of challenges never considered before, and a new set of rewards similarly never considered. Zinio's success is indicative of the extraordinary opportunity that exists in that virtual, magical space that allows content and ideas and dreams to flow so freely between so many people at once, and is no doubt, the way and the gold mine of the future.

The challenges that await with my newest start-up, Wakaya Perfection, fill me with the same thrill I have known so many times before—although this time the sensation is slightly different given my intentions with this particular company. Wakaya Perfection truly embodies the quest I have been on for the past eighty years—a quest for an understanding of the perfect product, of the sublime hopes and dreams that manifest in the most fundamental aspirations of people all around us, from all walks of life. As our world becomes more complex and polluted, as our lives take on ever-increasing complexities, we hunger (literally and figuratively) to feel better—to feel better about ourselves and what we utilise and consume. Basically, we each yearn for that which is perfect: the perfect organic food, the perfect organic drink, the perfect organic cosmetic (because some of us would like to look better, too!), as well as the perfect idyllic place with the perfect experience. It is that hunger and aspiration that I hope to sate with Wakaya Perfection. Once again, I am starting up. Lucky the man who is always beginning.

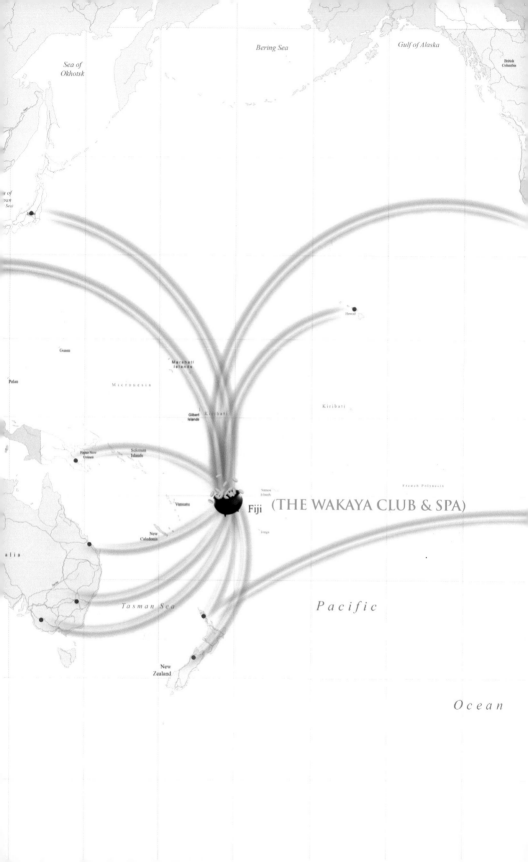

ISA LEI

> *"I am an optimist. It does not seem too much use being anything else."*
> —Sir Winston Churchill

THE ANCIENT EGYPTIAN SYMBOL OF LIFE, THE ANKH, has unknown origins. To this day, debate continues about its meaning and about how its meaning and purpose evolved as it passed down through the ages. It always seems absolutely appropriate to me that a symbol of life should be so shrouded in mystery. I can't think of anything more mysterious than life itself.

The ankh has always been a source of fascination to me—a symbol of the perpetuity of life's cycles. My interest, no doubt, has a good deal to do with my more than 50 trips to Egypt during the Pyramid Oasis days and with the deep impression President Anwar Sadat made on Peter Munk and me during our meetings with this extraordinary statesman and his ministers. Sadat's courage and his resolve, like the bravery of my own father when he crawled out at night to rescue his wounded comrades on the battlefields of the First World War, make me think of something Winston Churchill once said. It's advice that entrepreneurs would do well to remember when they encounter the inevitable fears and anxieties of a start-up: "One ought never to turn one's back on danger and try to run away from it. If you do that, you will double the danger. But if you meet it promptly and without flinching, you will reduce the danger by half. Never run away from anything. Never."

Had I not visited Egypt, and I had I not had the privilege of meeting with Anwar Sadat, the ankh would still hold a special meaning for me. I have learned that life and death, joy and grief, success and failure, discovery and loss are parts of the same graceful loop. As Steven Green wrote in his remarkable book, *Good Value*: "We know for sure that we will stumble but that remorse is always an option, and that atonement and renewal are always possible. Even when something feels like the end, it can be just the beginning."

What seem to be opposites can in fact contribute to the same ongoing process. It is because of the lessons this continuum teaches that I so often say that entrepreneurs are not born. They are born of life's experiences. The ankh illustrates this beautifully, simply, clearly.

To say that things happen for a reason is another way of saying that we are formed by all our experiences. Perhaps more than most other people, the entrepreneur knows this to be true. The ventures we undertake tomorrow are the result of ideas or observations or actions or relationships that had their beginnings in our past—sometimes in our distant past. Where would Peter Munk and I have ended up had Clairtone continued on from success to success? Would Jill and I have found our way to our satisfying and enriching commitment to preschool education as a way of honouring Erin's legacy had I not suffered the disappointment of those three miserable cheques for $100 in Lyford Cay? Our setbacks often point the way ahead. Large or small, important or trivial, public or personal, every memory we have is a clue to where we are going.

I've always taken the ankh to be symbolic of both eternity and the interconnectedness of life's experiences. I am drawn to the idea of the past having a relationship with the future—a belief that, in many ways, has guided me all my life.

Things connect. We don't always see what the connection will be, but if we pay attention to those elements of life that are truly important to us, past and future have a way of intertwining, like the curving lines of the ankh. In my study at our home in Palm Beach, there is a portrait of my father in his hunting pinks, painted by Cleeve Horne in 1947, and in the background are the fields of Far Hills, the farm outside Toronto where my family went on holidays and weekends to ride, and to fox hunt, and (for me, at any rate) to help with the hay and the barns and the stables. Now as I sit in my study (often on the phone, or on my computer, communicating with my team at Wakaya), I think to myself, how fascinating that the agricultural projects we are undertaking on Wakaya have returned me to my roots, to my love for Far Hills in my teenage years. And how fascinating that the disciplines and focus that we are bringing to the growing and harvesting of organic ginger and dilo, and the careful thinking that has gone into the marketing of the Wakaya Perfection suite of products, draw on the lessons learned from Clairtone, from FIJI Water, from *VIV* and Zinio.

"Stay focused," I hear myself saying to my Wakaya team. "Let's not run off in a dozen directions at once." And when I hear myself insisting on focus, on clarity, on defining exactly the niche in the marketplace that I want Wakaya Perfection to fill, I feel I am returning to lessons I learned long ago. When we are doing everything possible to hit that niche precisely with both our production and our marketing, I realize that my past is connecting with the present and with the future. There, before my very eyes, is the meaning of the ankh.

Scandinavian design or bottled water, hi-fi units or digital magazines, a resort and spa or the pure organic products of Wakaya Perfection—these seem to me to be cut from the same bolt of cloth. When we were developing the bottle and label for FIJI Water, it took us 32 tries before we got it right. We have agonized over the details of Wakaya Perfection with the same obsessive rigour.

"For the sake of the future, man shall honour the past. It will thus sanctify the present for him," are words written on a card we received from a friend, an officer in the Coldstream Guards, and although they were not written as advice for businessmen or entrepreneurs, that is what they can easily be seen to be. We make connections. We see our future in the lessons and experience of the past. We forget what we have done, where we have been, and who we have loved at our peril.

I am haunted by a memory of swimming with my father in the famous Blue Grotto in Capri. It was during our family summer holiday in 1937 when I was just six years old. A statue of myself at this age, also by Cleeve Horne, sits on a chest just outside my Palm Beach study, and the two portraits—one, a painting of my father, and the other, a life-size bust of me, both by the same artist—are in sight of one another. I imagine the memory of our swim to the Blue Grotto stays with me so vividly because it must have been one of the few times that I was alone with Dad.

He was a man of his time, much less actively involved in the raising of his children than fathers are today. But this distance made him seem all the more mythic a figure to me when I was a boy. He was the war hero who had been wounded several times while rescuing men from no-man's-land, and the recipient for these displays of bravery of the Military Cross and Bar. He was the successful businessman, the handsome, dashing sportsman, the rock of dependability, the source of sage advice and practical wisdom. I have no doubt that he had his foibles and his failings, as all humans do, but to a young boy, his son, these were not very apparent. He was a lofty example to be followed, a standard against which I always measured myself. And which, to be frank, I still do.

In my files, I have a letter I once sent to him—a letter, I was pleased to discover after his death, that he kept among his papers. "I enjoy hearing from you, Dad, very much. So when you have a moment drop me a line. Your advice and help have been so very wonderful. My greatest goal and desire is to repay you for all you have done in every way. All my love, your son."

How much of my success, I often wonder, has been my attempt to make this repayment? How much of what I have achieved is due to my aspiration to become the kind of man my father would admire and respect? How much of what I've accomplished, and what I will accomplish still, have their origins in whatever was going through a young boy's mind, on that summer's day, swimming with his father in that underwater cave in Capri?

Let me tell you about something that happened recently at the end of one couple's stay at The Wakaya Club and Spa—at the end of ten days of picnics on beautiful, entirely deserted beaches, mornings on the tennis court or golf course, afternoons spent snorkeling on the coral reefs directly in front of their seaside cottage-suite. The tradition at The Wakaya Club and Spa is that at the end of a stay, before our guests pack their bags and take the Cessna Grand Caravan eight-seater aircraft to the main island to catch the night flight back to Los Angeles, or to Vancouver, the staff gathers on the wooden terrace, beneath the spreading dilo tree, to sing a traditional Fijian song, "Isa Lei."

The Wakaya Club and Spa's staff, like almost all Fijians, are good singers, adept at haunting harmonies. They are sincerely hospitable and, while solicitous, are possessed of a quiet dignity. They are genuinely friendly. And in this instance, as Jill and I watched proudly, they were bidding our two departing guests goodbye. With a staff-to-guest ratio of 12 to one, the group gathered to sing farewell created a sizeable choir.

The Wakaya Club and Spa advertises itself by not advertising. Its fame spreads by word of mouth through the circles of those who can afford it and who appreciate its elegant simplicity and uncompromising standards. As Andrew Harper wrote in his *Hideaway Report*, "It is the thoughtful attention to detail that one marvels at most: the colourful lounging robes and slippers sized differently for men and women; the huge closets outfitted with proper wooden hangers for pants and skirts; straw sun hats and beach bags hanging on pegs by the door; the eclectic assortment of hardback classics and Fijian cultural books on the writing desk and coffee table; the welcome fruit and cheese platter on arrival; the jar of assorted homemade cookies; and on and on it goes."

The Wakaya Club's exotic location, its natural splendour, and its gentle climate have brought it to the attention of publications such as *Elle Décor*, *People*, *Departures*, *Town & Country*, *The New York Times*, *Condé Nast Traveller*, and *Travel + Leisure*. The elite circle who pay attention to Andrew Harper's *Hideaway Report* ("a connoisseur's worldwide guide to peaceful and unspoiled places") know that, in an extremely exclusive field, The Wakaya Club and Spa is very highly regarded indeed. "Embraced by shell-strewn beaches and azure lagoons, this enchanting and astonishingly scenic 2,200-acre island paradise comes enhanced by an exceptionally amiable staff."

As the staff assembled, our departing guests stood up from their table. They had enjoyed an al fresco luncheon of grilled lobster tails and a chilled bottle of New Zealand's finest Sauvignon Blanc, and now they found themselves facing the people who had attended them during their stay—and it was a magical moment.

Earlier that morning the couple had told me that against all odds—meaning, I took it, contrary to the prevailing trends of 21st-century tourism—their holiday had been everything they had hoped it would be. As a matter of fact, "perfect" was the word they used. They said their holiday had been—and here they bounced descriptions back and forth between themselves like a tennis ball—relaxing, adventurous, and romantic. It had been fun, restorative, refreshing, rejuvenating even. On their last day, they felt better—far healthier, far calmer, and far more energetic—than they had felt when they arrived.

I wasn't surprised. In fact, the change was perfectly obvious. It almost always is.

I occasionally like to take a photograph of the couples I know well, on their first day on Wakaya and on their last. "Before and after," I explain to them. And when I showed the couple their snapshots, it was, they had to admit, a remarkable transformation. They had relaxed and slept soundly during their holiday. They had paused, caught their breath, and remembered what was important. They had talked to one another about the kinds of things that the hectic rush of ordinary life often leaves no time for. They were different after. The island had changed them.

And I suppose it was because of this—because an expectation had been fulfilled, because the day was lovely, because their holiday had been perfect, and because the Fijians were singing so pretty and wistful a song—that something happened to that couple on the terrace that afternoon.

They were standing after their last lunch, listening. The tradition behind "Isa Lei" is that it must be sung as a farewell if a person is to return to the islands of Fiji. Its gentle sadness is infectious. At first I noticed that the man was looking a little uncomfortable. And then I realized that this was because, standing beside him, his wife was crying.

I do not mean a mere moistening of the eyes and a catch of the voice. She was sobbing, actually. And then she was laughing at herself for crying. And then she was sobbing some more.

The beautiful singing continued. So did the tears. The husband looked helpless. The departing couple's fellow guests looked on with a mixture of sympathy, concern, and affectionate amusement.

The song ended. The guests applauded the singers. The staff stepped forward to say goodbye to the couple. And the wife kept crying. And laughing. And crying.

"Don't worry," Jill said. Jill always knows exactly what to do. She left my side and rushed forward to give her tearful guest a comforting hug. "It happens quite often when people have to go."

It was Celine Dion who, after her visit to Wakaya, told *People* magazine, "When you leave you cry—because it is an experience out of the ordinary." Consequently, the SUV that transports our guests to their waiting flight is equipped with Kleenex boxes, front and back.

And now let me tell you something that happens to me. How many times have I departed Wakaya over the years? How many times have I listened to "Isa Lei," and bade farewell to our staff and friends? How many times have I boarded the Cessna Grand Caravan, made that same run down Wakaya's private airstrip, and looked from the window of the plane down on the island I love so much? You'd think I'd be inured to these departures. But no. Jill always looks over and smiles kindly. I smile back, always feeling a little embarrassed. Inevitably, one of us will start to cry. I'm always glad we keep those Kleenex boxes on the airplane that takes us away from what we hold so dear.

"It happens quite often when people have to go." Jill's kind, comforting comment is a sentence that takes on ever-increasing meaning the older I get. People do have to go—and many in my life, very sadly, have already done so. This, of course, is the only thing we know for certain: Change will always come. Sometimes without warning—like a phone call in the middle of the night. Sometimes slowly, gradually, almost imperceptibly—the way the sky and the sea change at dawn when I watch the light and colours shift from the deck of Sega na Leqa. The name means "no worries" in Fijian.

With the constancy of change very much in mind, I've hired Russell Thornley to assist me in my vision for agricultural sustainability on the island. I consider this my last start-up—the raising and harvesting of all organic produce, nurtured in virgin, volcanic soil, rich in nutrients. These are products that are part of my plan to make Wakaya self-sustaining and that continue the legacy of health and well-being that are so integral to our Wakaya life. I watch the ginger grow with the same pride and excitement I felt when Peter Munk and I looked at the first Clairtone model. I marshal my ideas and hopes for ginger, and dilo oil, and for all the produce we raise on Wakaya with the same enthusiasm that first set me on my course as a businessman and entrepreneur.

Sustainability, purity and effectiveness—words that so often are bandied about so carelessly—they are what must lie at the core of business ventures today. We do not have time to imagine otherwise—the days of the disposable product and the disposable politician are close to being gone forever. The story of Noah's ark has always been one of my favourites—and I can't help but feel that the ark is an apt metaphor for what we are creating. The floods of environmental degradation, of crass commercialization, political upheaval, social unrest, and economic uncertainty rise, and we are building a ship that will guard what we love from the stormy seas ahead. I sometimes feel as if we are setting sail on the last bastion of sanity in a world gone mad.

Wakaya's interior has concealed valleys ideal for organic

fruits and vegetables. The grass and coconut are ideal feed for our organically raised poultry, lamb, and venison, but our guests at The Wakaya Club and Spa will be entirely oblivious to this production. It will be an environmentally sensitive, highly controlled operation, fully in accord with the preservation of the island's natural beauty and with The Wakaya Club and Spa's emphasis on uncompromised excellence. Such delicacies as our own organic venison and our Muscovy duck will be served to our guests. Under our agriculture manager's expert guidance we have been raising our own organically fed chicken, deer, Fiji Fantastic sheep—as well as potatoes, lime, pineapples, avocado, carrots, beans, and six varieties of lettuce. Our organically grown papaya—a delicious fruit abundant in antioxidants—is a pure delight to eat. We are only beginning to learn about the many beneficial and healthful qualities of our ginger—ginger that is, I have no doubt, the best in the world. And as I sit here, in Sega na Leqa, looking out to the blue Koro Sea, it makes me smile to think that all this—this emphasis on health, and excellence, and on sustainability—will continue long after I am gone, and long after my name is forgotten. This natural abundance will be carefully nurtured and maintained and the beauty of the island I love so much will be preserved—all because of a memory I have of a tousle-haired girl running carefree along its beaches.

During that family summer holiday long ago, I was keen to explore the famous underwater cave in Capri that my parents had told me about. So Dad and I swam to the Blue Grotto. It seemed a great adventure. And by happenstance, no other swimmers were there at the time. We swam and treaded water. We talked, our voices echoing. It was just the two of us. I remember our arms sparkled with phosphorescence as we moved together through the mysterious blue light.

FIN